THE
CULINARY
BRO-DOWN

COOKBOOK

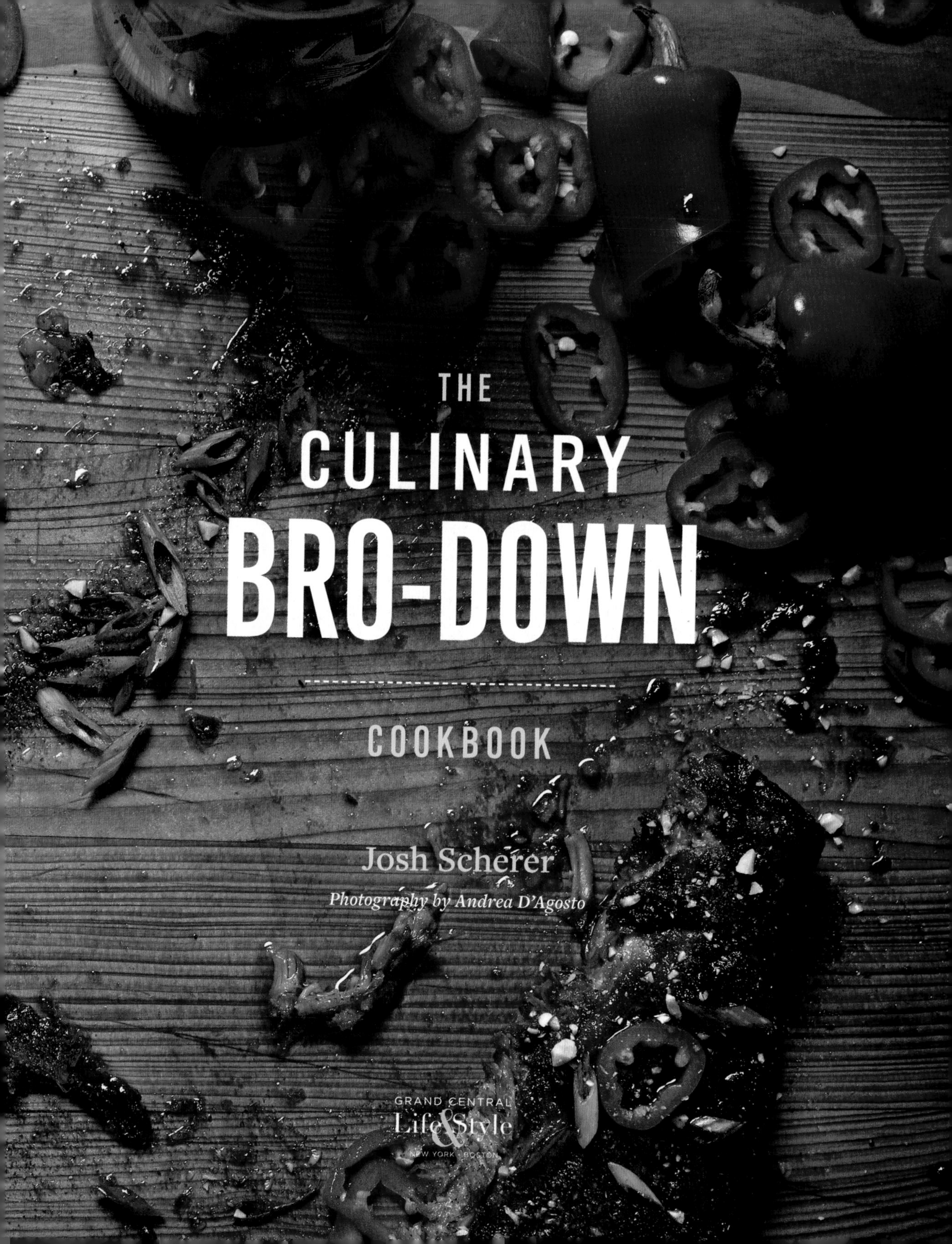

THE
CULINARY
BRO-DOWN

COOKBOOK

Josh Scherer

Photography by Andrea D'Agosto

GRAND CENTRAL
Life & Style
NEW YORK • BOSTON

Grand Central Life & Style

Hachette Book Group

1290 Avenue of the Americas, New York, NY 10104

grandcentrallifeandstyle.com

twitter.com/grandcentralpub

First Edition: August 2017

Grand Central Life & Style is an imprint of Grand Central Publishing. The Grand Central Life & Style name and logo are trademarks of Hachette Book Group, Inc.

The publisher is not responsible for websites (or their content) that are not owned by the publisher.

The Hachette Speakers Bureau provides a wide range of authors for speaking events. To find out more, go to www.hachettespeakersbureau.com or call (866) 376-6591.

Food Stylist: Lauren Anderson StoneColdSyleLA

Prop Stylist: Alicia Buszczak

Surfaces and Props Provided by: The Surface Library

Library of Congress Cataloging-in-Publication Data

Names: Scherer, Josh, author. | D'Agosto, Andrea, photographer.
Title: The culinary bro-down cookbook / Josh Scherer ; photography by Andrea D'Agosto.
Description: First edition. | New York : Grand Central Life & Style, [2017] | Includes index.
Identifiers: LCCN 2017008851| ISBN 978-1-4555-9542-6 (hardcover) | ISBN 978-1-4555-9543-3 (ebook)
Subjects: LCSH: Cooking, American. | LCGFT: Cookbooks.
Classification: LCC TX715 .S145323 2017 | DDC 641.5973—dc23
LC record available at https://lccn.loc.gov/2017008851

ISBNs: 978-1-4555-9542-6 (hardcover); 978-1-4555-9543-3 (ebook)

Printed in the United States of America

Q-MA

10 9 8 7 6 5 4 3 2 1

To my dad, **RUSSEL,** may he rest in peace. No matter how stupid my dreams were, he always encouraged me to chase them. **To my brother, JON,** who's always been there for me. **And to ANDREA,** because without her I'd be gnawing on half-eaten Slim Jims in a dumpster somewhere.

INTRODUCTION

In the Beginning

We worshipped our grill like a deity that summer; it was our 60,000 BTU, child-labor-made Aztec sun god. Whoever got up the earliest on any given day, generally sometime around noon, was given the responsibility of cranking all six burners on high. The grill bled propane into the sky for ten hours a day.

ALL OUR CLOTHES SMELLED LIKE SMOKE, BURNT ANIMAL FAT, and stale beer. We couldn't have given less fucks if we tried.

Did I need 800 degrees of open flame to make scrambled eggs for breakfast? Probably not. Was the grill a gross example of overconsumption? Bet your ass it was, but it was *our* gross example of overconsumption. For the first time in our lives we owned something more permanent than an Xbox, and we were going to run it into the ground.

There were ten of us dude-bros and one dog living in a four-bedroom duplex in Isla Vista, the beachside shantytown next to University of California, Santa Barbara. I think it's legally considered a slum based on the disease rates, crime rates, and population density. But if you have to live in a slum, it might as well be one with thousands of beautiful people and private beach access.

Our lawn was just big enough to fit that big-dicked grill and a 12-foot-long conference table used exclusively for drinking games and ritualistic hungover brunches. Partygoers flooded the streets every Friday night while we hung out on the lawn grilling up sausages, selling them to anyone who inquired for $5 apiece.

It may not have been the Culinary Institute of America, or Le Cordon Bleu, or even a minimum-wage job washing dishes at a TGI Friday's, but this summer of wine-in-a-can debauchery taught me more about food than the previous two decades combined. My parents didn't cook, I have no ancestral background to draw from, and I never volunteered in soup kitchens to experience the communal splendor of nourishment or whatever.

Did I need 800 DEGREES
of open flame to
make scrambled eggs
for breakfast?
Probably not.

Josh at the grill making ◄ **KOREAN SKIRT STEAK, PAGE 163**

Instead, I drank and cooked and dicked around with my friends. We made 12-pound pork roasts with roasted tomatillo puree, bacon marmalade burgers, *tortilla españolas,* rum hams (both attempts inedible)—all cooked by that magnificently powerful but shoddily assembled extension of our collective manhood parked in the front yard.

When most food writers describe their epiphany moment—the single instance that defined their perspective on food, when they decided it was more important than anything in the world—few talk about Natty Light binges and pizza-pocket-filled monstrosities.

Most talk about their mother's hands as she kneaded pasta dough; each crevice engraved in her palm a moment frozen in time, an annal, a rich cultural dialogue immortalized in bowls of misshapen cavatelli. Or how the peach tree in their childhood backyard stood as a metaphor for lost innocence. And that's totally cool, for them. I just had different experiences.

My mom ashed a cigarette into our Rice-A-Roni when I was a kid on more than one occasion. It's not a metaphor, it just made our dinner taste like Camel Blue Wides. Sometimes she'd forget to go shopping and we'd eat boiled potatoes with ketchup for dinner.

McDonald's used to have this promotion for 39-cent cheeseburgers every Sunday, limit ten per customer. My dad would have my brother and me wait in separate lines and order ten burgers each so we could throw them in the freezer back home and have freshly microwaved dinners for the week. I got so scared that McDonald's was onto our scheme that one day I refused to go in the store and was left hysterically crying in the car.

When I talk about chugging beers and drunk cooking in the middle of parties and making obscene foods that most rational people would consider abominations of God, it's important that you know it's not for shock, or effect, or novelty. In no superficial way, these are all the happiest, most important moments of my life.

THE 13 CULINARY
BROMMANDMENTS

1
BACON IS GOOD; PORK BELLY IS BETTER.

If you're not previously familiar with the merits of bacon, get out. Get the hell out and never come back, just like my stepdad. But, if bacon is good, pork belly is stealing-your-roommate's-Brazzers-password good. It's just giant, do-it-yourself bacon, which lends itself to all kinds of possibilities: beer-braised bacon, fish-sauce-caramel bacon, caffeinated bacon. The world is your oyster, covered in bacon.

2
MAKE COCKTAILS IN DIET COKE CANS.

Take those empty Diet Coke cans that you have lying around and fill them with liquor and other mixers—soda, fruit, hot sauce—then shake until it's a cocktail. This way, while you're playing drunk badminton on your lawn, you can violently gesture at your teammate for fucking up that serve without spilling your hard-earned liquor.

3
TACOS ARE A SMART LIFESTYLE DECISION.

Tacos are the Diet Coke cans of food. They're completely self-contained, everything you could ever want or need is wrapped up in an edible little handkerchief, and the flavor combinations therein are endless. If you're going into a sporting event, music festival, bar mitzvah, etc., line your pockets with tacos to make sure you get your daily macronutrients.

4
LOVE ISN'T A FUCKING INGREDIENT.

Using love as your secret ingredient is incredibly similar to using nothing as your secret ingredient. In fact, I think some people must be lying about their recipes and products, because I've never been able to taste it. I wrote a series of complaints to the FDA but they must not have gotten them, because I've heard nothing back. But seriously, your final product tastes like a combination of your ingredients and process, no love involved, so get that innocuous, overwrought garbage out of your head.

5
ANYTHING CAN BE DORITO-CRUSTED.

You can deep-fry anything with a little hard work, ingenuity, and six pounds of beef tallow; and if you can deep-fry anything, you can sure as hell Dorito-crust anything. Freeze tomato soup in an ice cube tray, then beer-batter, Dorito-crust, and flash-fry those soupy bad boys for a drunken riff on a childhood classic.

6
EMPTY BEER BOTTLES ARE MULTIFACETED COOKING TOOLS.

I believe in recycling, but not in the traditional take-your-cans-to-a-recycling-plant kind of way. I believe in a more practical, guerrilla kind of recycling. Instead of throwing away your empty beer bottles, use them to improve your quality of culinary life. A bottle can be a rolling pin, a meat mallet, a tiny donut hole cutter; hell, I know a guy who will make it into a bong for $20.

7
FOOD IS THE BEST APHRODISIAC—OTHER THAN TIGER PENIS.

For those times when you don't have access to fresh or dried tiger penis, try making your significant other, or the person you're casually hooking up with, a nice dinner. It's a sexful gesture of supplication, it's a chance to prove that you're not a bumbling incompetent, and it gives you an excuse to poach cherries in red wine and shit. These are all ostensibly good things.

8
BAKING BLOWS.

This has nothing to do with preconceived gender stereotypes or threats to your masculinity; baking blows because it's difficult. Everything has to be measured and temperature controlled and you need to be generally knowledgeable about things—not worth it in the least. Instead, make desserts you can splash liquor at and light on fire. That way, people will think you're dangerous, and you get to consume alcohol.

9
EATING YOUR DRINKS MAKES YOU DOUBLE DRUNK.

Sneaking alcohol into your normal foods allows you to increase your potential maximum drunkenness (PMD). The easiest way is to substitute all your braising, stewing, and saucing liquids with beer; beer still retains 25 percent of

alcohol content after simmering for an hour, so eat up. But there's no wrong way to booze up your food. Start experimenting by pouring a shot of grain alcohol on your normal meals.

10
SALT EVERYTHING.

To undersalt deliberately in the name of dietary chic is to omit from the music of cookery the indispensable bass line over which all tastes and smells form their harmonies.
—ROBERT FARRAR CAPON

I plan on getting this tattooed in the shape of a spork on my forearm. Salt is the most important ingredient in your pantry (other than love), and it should be used with recklessly altruistic abandon.

11
VEGETABLES TASTE GOOD; DON'T BE A MORON.

Even though hot sauce should cover 50 to 70 percent of your daily vitamin intake, it shouldn't be used as an excuse to not eat real vegetables. Vegetables are great. People have a negative attitude towards them because they insist on steaming them like an asshole, but if you roast anything with olive oil, salt, and pepper, it's going to work out fine. Eat a fucking parsnip, bro.

12
BAGGED WINE IS THE ONLY WINE YOU NEED.

As a fiscally responsible adult, it's your duty to yourself, your progeny, and society at large to save money and invest in retirement plans, college funds, and I don't know, jet skis and shit. One easy way to save money is to avoid anything that requires a corkscrew; those things tend to be expensive. Instead, buy a five-liter bag of wine and pour it into old, fancy wine bottles on an ad hoc basis. No one will ever know.

13
DICK-SHAPED FOODS APLENTY.

This is more a rote observation than an actual suggestion, but all the best foods are shaped like dicks, and it's hilarious. Corn dogs, Fudgsicles, egg rolls, burritos—they're all unmistakably phallic and reaffirm that overbearing sense of masculinity your stomach subconsciously craves.

Kitchen
HANDBOOK

There are a few essential kitchen tools you'll need before embarking on this liquor-and-animal-fat-fueled food journey. Since cooking is all about accuracy, precision, and consistency, you'll need to purchase top-of-the-line equipment to set yourself up for success.

A Cuisinart food processor, Viking range, Le Creuset Dutch oven, one of those fridges that look like cabinets but they're actually fridges—you're going to need to buy all these things, immediately. Seriously, why are you still reading and not at Costco buying a three-pack of food dehydrators right now?

Psych! I own a grand total of none of these things, and I never intend to own most of them. Except for one of those secret camouflage fridges, those seem pretty rad. Imagine how safe your snacks would be if no one could find them but you...

I've never owned a stand mixer, hand mixer, rolling pin, steamer, rice cooker, deep fryer (OK, I had one for a month, but it was a total nightmare), or a pan that cost more than $29.99. All these things are wholly unnecessary if you know the right techniques to get around them. If you can get inside these simple machines' heads—if you can find out what makes them tick—you can master their basic operations. You can become the (wait for it) ultimate machine.

Every recipe in this book can be made using the following eight fun and frugal kitchen hacks, and the extra money you save can go towards a worthy cause. Let's not kid ourselves—you're going to use it for beer.

1

INSTEAD OF A
**ROLLING PIN,
USE AN EMPTY
WINE BOTTLE.**

First things first; drink that bottle of wine, champ, you earned it. Second thing, you better be rolling out pasta dough because otherwise you're on your way to violating Culinary Brommandment number 8: Baking blows. Drop the parchment paper and dough cutter, bro. If you rub flour on the wine bottle, it won't stick to your dough and you can use it just like a rolling pin. A quick note: This is exclusive to wine bottles. Wine bags and boxes—though ideal for drinking—will not yield similar results.

2

INSTEAD OF A
**BISCUIT CUTTER,
USE AN EMPTY
BEER BOTTLE.**

Unless you're Colonel Sanders—and I hope you are—and your livelihood depends on the rate at which your employees churn out uniform circles of dough, you don't really need a biscuit cutter. (Also, Mr. Colonel, if you do read this, I'm a huge fan of your work on the Double Down.) You already know how I feel about baking, but you get a pass on biscuits because they're stupid easy to make and their most immediate pairing is with fried chicken and/or gravy. Objection sustained. Press the beer bottle gently on the surface of your dough and follow the curvature with a paring knife for perfectly uniform cuts.

3

INSTEAD OF A
**MEAT MALLET,
USE AN
EMPTY VODKA
BOTTLE.**

Empty alcohol bottles make up at least 85 percent of my kitchen arsenal at this point. I'm still trying to find a way to make a stand mixer with a case of D batteries and a six-pack of Mike's Hard. It can be done. It must be done. Wrap your piece of meat in plastic wrap—or shove it into a gallon-size Ziploc bag—to avoid damaging the flesh, then gently beat the shit out of it with a bottle until it's at the desired thinness. I've also found that using your fists works shockingly well. I actually prefer it now. When your hands are in direct contact with the meat, you can really get a better feel for evenness. Either way, the choice is up to you. I'm not going to be like Ice Cube's dad in *Friday* and demand that you use your fists.

4

INSTEAD OF AN
**EXPENSIVE FOOD
PROCESSOR,
GET A CHEAP-ASS
BLENDER.**

Any liquid you would buzz up in a food processor you can also throw into any free blender you found on Craigslist. I still use my free Internet blender that I got six years ago—thanks, Craig! Alternatively, you could buy an immersion blender for as little as $10. Cheap food processors tend to break more easily than a blender because they have multiple moving parts. Plus, the free blender I got has one of those dispenser nozzles that come in handy when you're trying to serve piña coladas en masse.

☞ **TURN THE PAGE FOR ADDITIONAL ESSENTIAL TIPS**

Cheap-ass blender ←

5
INSTEAD OF AN EXPENSIVE FOOD PROCESSOR, TOUGH IT OUT AND USE A KNIFE.

Any solid you would throw into a food processor you can chop just as fine with a chef's knife and a bit of athleticism. You don't know your limits until you've surpassed them, and you don't know hand cramps until you've hand-chopped parsley for 50 portions of pistou. It builds character. And I actually mean this. It's super-important to learn your way around a chef's knife. When you get comfortable chopping things by hand, you're going to get faster and more efficient at literally every other knife cut. Yeah, practice. I'm talking about practice. Not a game. But practice. Think of something inspirational a mentor once said to you, then imagine that I said it instead, and start chopping.

6
INSTEAD OF A DEEP FRYER, USE A SAUCEPOT.

As someone who has successfully deep-fried ramen donuts, Dorito-crusted egg yolks, whole Chipotle burritos, and an entire ice cream cake, this is one of the few subjects that I'm truly qualified to speak on. Unless you buy a high-quality deep fryer, which might run you up to $200, they tend to be shoddily made and inaccurate. You're better off using a deep saucepot made from a heavy material so it can distribute heat evenly. I've been using a cast-iron Dutch oven that I got in a two-piece set for $29.99 for the past five years and I've never looked back. If you so choose, you can buy a thermometer, which is likely a good idea if you're new to frying. But I'll cover that in the next hack.

7
INSTEAD OF A FOOD THERMOMETER, TRUST YOUR INSTINCTS.

Cooking is less about times, temperatures, and measurements, and more about trust, instincts, and being a functioning person who can read visual cues. If you see oil smoking, it's too hot; if you drop a pinch of flour in and it doesn't sizzle, it's too cold. If a sauce isn't reducing, turn the heat up; if it's scalding and boiling over, turn it down. It's like playing free safety in the NFL—read the play and react—except it's a lot lamer, and you go to jail when you get caught with 12 grams of marijuana. Nothing in this book is too exact, and that's by design. I'm not a French chef who has the world's best pommes frites recipe timed down to the millisecond. I'm just some asshole throwing Tater Tots around and hoping I can give you some new ideas for what to do with them. As long as the oil is anywhere between 325 and 400°F, those tots are going to get crispy.

8
INSTEAD OF A GRILL... NOTHING! INSTEAD OF A GRILL, BUY A GRILL, DUMMY.

This one is nonnegotiable; you need a grill. If you don't already have one and money is tight, just drop your auto insurance plan for three months and save up; what's the worst that could happen? (Please do not do this.) There are no comparable substitutes for the charred flavor that comes with cooking things directly over fire, the way food messiah Bobby Flay intended. Both charcoal and gas have equal merits in terms of flavor and convenience, so I'll leave that decision up to you.

1

Beer

A GUIDE TO
LIGHT BEER
Tasting Notes

▶ If you're at a place in your life where you can fit smoked milk stouts, organic maple macadamia porters, and double dry-hopped XPAs into your normal day-to-day drinking habit, then by all means, you do you.

And I'll be right there by your side, slamming one of those maple macadamia joints and probably enjoying the hell out of it before eventually slipping out the back door and grabbing a 12-pack of Busch Light. Craft beer is great—we should all be supporting small businesses—and I've had a few microbrews that were mind-bendingly good, but there's something about the low stakes of conglomerate-made light beer that always seems to pull me back in.

Maybe it's just the nostalgia from college still barking at me like the junkyard dog that it is. Or maybe it's that drinking craft beer becomes a nerve-racking pissing contest (yeah, man, I totally get that piney mouthfeel, for sure), and most times when I'm drinking beer, I just want to drink a beer. Maybe I have truly abhorrent taste and am in no way qualified to give my opinion on beers, or anything for that matter. We'll never know.

That said, if you're a well-trained amateur drinker with a heart of gold like myself, you can notice the subtle differences between light beers and use those to your advantage when pairing with food and/or major life events. Here's what to look for in the perfect light beer.

BOUQUET: *Bouquet* is a fancy word for "smell." The fancier the adjective you throw at your beer, the more valuable it will be perceived by other people, and that's a point that should never be neglected. When observing the aroma of a light beer, you need to simplify your expectations; otherwise, you'll be off on a wild-goose chase looking for "overripe black fruit" and "mineral noses"— whatever the hell those mean. Light beer has two main smells: good and bad. Got a light beer that smells like your gym bag? No problem! Just pair it with the gnarliest, heaviest flavors you know of (See: Pork Belly Tacos with Fish Sauce Caramel on page 147).

HEAD: They say the best beers have such a thick, foamy head that a bottle cap will float on top without sinking. They've obviously never played Beer Pong. You don't have time to deal with a foamy head: Your team's down by three cups, you've used all your re-racks, and you refuse to put down your fish taco while you play the game, because fish tacos always take priority. ALWAYS. You want the least foamy head possible so you can focus on more important things. Make sure you test the head on a Solo cup and not glass, because certain beers fizz more aggressively than others while interacting with the chemical coating on the plastic.

COLOR: You're looking for anywhere between a pale, translucent yellow and a pale, translucent amber—the translucence is really key here. Personally, I always abide by the newspaper test. Take the sports page, which is the only page you should be reading in a newspaper—all your current events should come from Tweetstorms and BuzzFeed character quizzes—and hold it behind your glass of light beer. If you can read an NBA box score through your beer, then it's light enough for you to drink. Anything darker than that and the flavor will detract from your meal.

SMOOTHNESS: If you ever find yourself at a wine tasting—and I hope you don't, unless you've managed to sneak in your own flask of Kool-Aid and grain alcohol—you'll learn that you're generally asked to judge wine while stone-cold sober. This just doesn't seem practical to me. A light beer's smoothness isn't crucial during the first sip; it's crucial during the thousandth sip. You never want to be caught 14-deep and dreading the next sip because you chose an unsmooth light beer. Rookie move. The smoothest beers typically have high translucence and a "good" to "medium good" bouquet.

Shotgunning

DRUNKENING COEFFICIENT: This is the most important bro-math you'll ever do in your life. Take the alcohol percentage of the beer, divide it by cost per beer, then multiply the product by its smoothness breaking point (the number of beers you can get through without dreading the next one).

Let's look at an example. Bud Light Platinum is 6 percent ABV (alcohol by volume), costs $1.23 per beer, and you can drink about 11 until the taste gets completely unbearable. That yields a drunkening coefficient (DC) of 53.6—not a terrible score. But compare that to Natural Light, which has 4.2 percent ABV, costs $.49 per beer, and has a unique water-like taste that gives it a smoothness breaking point of 16. That yields a DC of 137.1, which is the highest currently on record.

Every recipe in this chapter is designed for you to explore your way through the nuances and complexities of light beer. For instance, harness the stank-ass bouquet of Miller Lite to cut through the sweetness of caramel sauce. Embrace the high drunkening coefficient of Natty to stretch your dollar even further with Grilled-Pineapple Beergria. Buy up a few 30-racks, and open your mind and kitchen to the endless culinary possibilities of light beer.

BEER-BRINED PORK BELLY CUBANOS

SERVES 4

2 cans of your favorite light beer

2 cups orange juice

¼ cup lime juice

3 tablespoons chopped garlic

2 tablespoons ground cumin

2 tablespoons salt

1 tablespoon cracked black pepper

3- to 4-pound slab boneless skinless pork belly

2 baguettes

¼ cup yellow mustard

1 pound thin-sliced deli ham (spring for some good shit)

4 slices white American cheese (way better than Swiss)

4 thin slices pickled green tomato (or regular dill pickles, whatevs)

2 tablespoons unsalted butter

There's nothing wrong with a standard Cuban sandwich, and I'm not saying the alterations I've made are necessarily improvements on a dish rooted in history, except they totally are. First, sub out that easy-to-fuck-up pork shoulder with hard-to-fuck-up pork belly. You'll be grateful for the extra fat in there, trust me. You're going to be brining it for 12 hours, which, I get it—that sucks—but it's totally worth it, and you will look back on this recipe and thank me one day. Second, replace Swiss cheese with its creamier, more processed counterpart, white American. Any time you can increase the meltiness factor of a dish, I say go for it. Third, slap some slices of pickled green tomato (the brand Bubbies makes a great pickle) on there instead of your typical dill pickles. If you're not already on this pickled-green-tomato-hype train, you need to jump on real fast.

---

1 Whisk together your beer, orange juice, lime juice, garlic, cumin, salt, and pepper in a bowl large enough to fit the pork belly.

2 Put the pork belly in the bowl and use your hands to massage the marinade into the meat—get in there all nice and deep-like. Then seal the bowl with plastic wrap and throw it in the fridge. Flip the meat every 6 hours and make sure it marinates for at least 12.

3 Preheat your oven to 400°F. Take the pork belly out of the marinade and wipe off any chunks that might be sticking to it. Put a roasting rack on top of a baking sheet, toss the pork belly on there, and put it in the oven.

4 Bake for 1 hour, then, when the marinade has started to caramelize and the pork is browned, drop the temp down to 275°F and bake for another 2½ hours, until the pork is fully cooked and fork tender. The low temp is going to help the fat render.

5 Take the pork belly out of the oven and let it rest at room temp for at least 20 minutes. Take a dangerously sharp knife that you probably shouldn't be trusted to handle—but, hey, I'm still here—and slice the pork belly as thinly as possible. It's going to start flaking a little, but that doesn't matter. Roll with the punches.

6 Cut the baguettes in half lengthwise, then in half… Widthwise? Lay down a solid schmear of mustard on the cut sides. Top with pork belly, ham (ratio should be 2:1, belly to ham), American cheese, and pickled green tomato, then pop that top bread on.

7 So I'd just heat a half tablespoon of butter in a large sauté pan on medium heat, then, when it's melted, throw a sandwich on there—work one half-baguette sandwich at a time—and use a saucepot to press it down. Griddle it off for about 3 minutes on one side, or until golden brown, then flip and do the same for the second side. Add more butter to the pan and repeat the process for each sandwich.

8 Enjoy with an ice-cold trash beer.

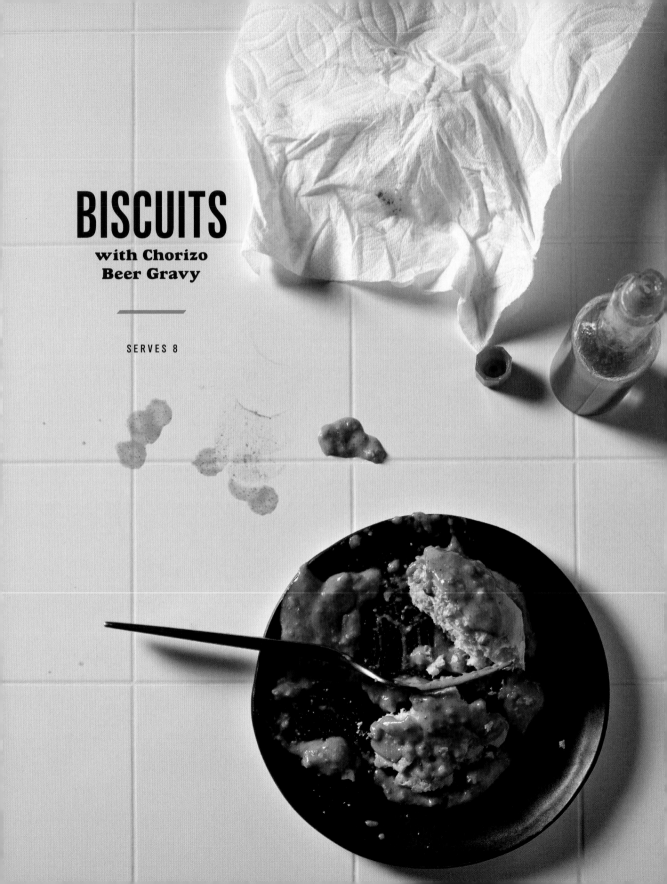

BISCUITS

with Chorizo Beer Gravy

SERVES 8

If you will, kindly consult the Culinary Brommandment number 8: Baking blows. Note that the rule, as written, is only explicitly related to desserts. In fact, one could also make the argument that—due to a complete lack of attention to detail in the wording—Brommandment number 8 is specific to ornate pastries.

Ugh, fuck, fine, you got me, those rules mean nothing. As far as baking things go though, biscuits are probably the best thing to start out with. They literally take you less than half an hour from start to cleanup and they require almost no skill or attention to detail. They're cheat code pastries. They're the baked goods that turn off the offsides penalty on Madden and just let you fucking massacre the QB every play.

However, there are a few rules you have to remember: Don't overmix your dough, and don't ever let the butter get warm. Keep that shit freezing cold. But even if you do that, you're drowning the whole thing in a bunch of pork fat and beer, so it doesn't even matter if you completely fuck it up. I mean, still try not to, but with a safety net like that, you might as well. That said, if you want to scrap all that completely and use premade biscuit dough from a can, I will not judge you.

Biscuits

¾ stick (6 tablespoons) butter

2 cups flour

4 teaspoons baking powder

½ teaspoon baking soda

1 teaspoon salt, plus more for seasoning

2 tablespoons lard

1 cup buttermilk

4 tablespoons butter, melted

Gravy

8 ounces of the fattiest chorizo you can find, Cacique brand or similar (see step 8)

2 tablespoons flour

2 cans light beer of your choice

Salt

Hot sauce, for serving

1 For the biscuits: Preheat your oven to 400°F. Dust a baking sheet with flour. Take the ¾ stick of butter and put it in the freezer for at least half an hour. You want to make a butter Popsicle—but don't eat it! I know it's tempting, but remember all that abstinence-only education you got in school and use that to help you control your urges.

2 In a large mixing bowl, throw together the flour, baking powder, baking soda, and salt and whisk.

3 Cube up that butter Popsicle. Cube it real tiny. And remember, you need to make sure the butter stays frozen when you incorporate it into the dough because when it melts you want it to create air pockets in the biscuit. Or something? Dude, I really don't know, baking is hard. This is all just shit I remember from having the Food Network on as background noise for thousands of hours in my life.

4 Use your hands to gently mix the butter and lard into the dry ingredients, making sure to mash it ever so slightly, but not so much that the butter melts.

5 Dump all that shit onto a giant cutting board, or you can just use your counter if it's clean. Or if it's not. This has no effect on me. Make a well in the middle of your buttery flour and pour the buttermilk into it. Mix the flour into the buttermilk gradually with your hands, working quickly and gently and sensually so the butter doesn't melt.

Recipe Continues ☞

6 Use a rolling pin (aka an old wine bottle or full tallboy) to roll out the dough into a 1-inch-thick sheet. Then use a biscuit cutter (old whiskey glass) to cut the dough into 3- or 4-inch rounds.

7 Toss them fatty dough pucks onto that floured baking sheet and brush the tops with the melted butter. Bake at 400°F for 12 to 15 minutes, until golden brown.

8 **For the gravy:** You want to get a Mexican brand of chorizo, and none of that artisanal shit. I'm talking big-brand chorizo, like Cacique. The stuff made with lymph nodes and salivary glands—that's a real thing! If your stuff comes in a casing, de-case it. Heat a large sauté pan on medium-high heat and throw in the chorizo. Use a wooden spoon to break up the sausage bits. Sauté for 6 or 7 minutes, until a whole lot of fat has rendered and the chorizo is looking a little crispy. Add in that 2 tablespoons of flour and stir to combine. Let cook for another 2 minutes until the flour gets roasty.

9 Pour in half of the beer and crank the heat to high. Whisk to incorporate, and, when the mixture starts to thicken and bubble, add in the second can of beer and continue to whisk.

10 Keep stirring as the mixture eventually comes to a boil. You need to cook it down to get that raw beer stink out. This'll take about 10 minutes, until the mixture has reduced by half and the consistency resembles, you know, gravy. Turn the heat off and add salt to taste, but the amount you need is really going to vary based on how salty your chorizo is.

11 Pour the beer gravy on the biscuits. Add hot sauce. Add more hot sauce. Spoon gravy directly into your mouth. Shotgun a beer. Cry in a corner. Eat a biscuit.

WHIZ-LIT
CHEESESTEAKS

MAKES 4 SANDWICHES

2 pounds ribeye steaks (get the cheapest you can find; don't be a hero)

1 large white onion

2 tablespoons vegetable oil

2 tablespoons butter

1 tablespoon flour

1 can light beer

½ cup heavy cream

8 ounces yellow American cheese

1 tablespoon nutritional yeast (optional, but recommended because it'll make your whiz taste exponentially cheesier)

1 teaspoon mustard powder (also optional, but, come on, man, just do it; do me a solid on this)

1 teaspoon ground turmeric (again, you don't have to do anything you don't want to do, but Jesus, will you just trust me? For once?)

4 hoagie rolls

Cherry peppers from a jar

Salt

I am very proud of the name of this dish, but I fear it may need a brief explainer. You see, in Philadelphia, there is a popular sandwich known as a "cheesesteak." A common way to order a cheesesteak—some would say the *only* way—is with Cheez Whiz and onions. This gets abbreviated to "Whiz-with," but pronounced as if it were spelled "Whiz-wit." My cheese-steak is called the "Whiz-*Lit*," because "lit" was once common parlance for "fucked up"—remember, the recipe is made with beer—before it started meaning whatever the fuck it means today. Great, so we're squared away then.

Nothing can compete with whiz on cheesesteaks, and I can confirm that this is the only proper and true way to order a cheesesteak. White American puts up a little bit of a challenge, but, still, it's not that close. Here I tried my best to create a version of that perma-liquid cheese spread, except also using beer. It's easy to get the taste right; the hard part is getting that signature, violently yellow hue. That's where ground turmeric comes into play. If you don't already have it, you should **really** invest in a bottle—it costs $6 and it will give you an eternity of turning shit yellow.

1 Put the steaks in the freezer for at least an hour. The key to making a Philly cheesesteak that doesn't taste like some Denny's-ass bullshit is being able to slice the steak super thin when it's raw and then murdering it in a hot pan. Philly cheesesteaks with chunky beef are trash. Freezing the beef is going to let you slice it thinner, and not be a total fuck-up at life.

2 While the cow parts are getting nice and chilly, dice that onion. Heat 1 tablespoon of the vegetable oil in a large sauté pan on medium heat. When it's hot, throw in your onions and sauté for about 10 minutes. You really don't want too much color on them, and you sure as shit don't want to caramelize them. Your goal is for pure, sweaty translucence. Set aside.

3 Heat a medium saucepot on medium heat and add the butter. When it's melted, add the flour and stir in with a wooden spoon. When the flour turns a nice golden color, after about 2 minutes, add the beer and cream and whisk. Bring that mixture up to a bubble. Let it reduce for 3 minutes while continuing to whisk. Gotta cook off the beer stank. Add the cheese, and, if you did the one fucking thing I asked you to do, the nutritional yeast, mustard powder, and turmeric (for the yellow). When the cheese is melted and the mixture is homogeneous, turn off the heat and let the whiz hang out.

4 You can probably take those steaks out of the freezer now. You don't want them to be rock solid, because that would make slicing impossible, but you also don't want them to be just chilled. You need some frozen texture in there.

Recipe Continues 👉

5 Sharpen your knife as sharp as it will sharpen. Hattori Hanzo shit. Slice through the ribeyes against the grain of fat as thinly as you can. It sucks because there's no shortcut here, but you gotta do it. Put the team on your back, youngblood!

6 Heat the remaining 1 tablespoon vegetable oil in a heavy-bottomed sauté pan—or cast-iron skillet—on the highest heat you can find. Make that shit NaPoM hot (not a misspelling of the incendiary weapon used to commit war crimes in Vietnam, but professional beatboxer NaPoM. Dude is absolute fire).

7 **IMPORTANT STEP:** While the pan is heating up, slice the hoagie rolls in half but leave the hinges intact. Schmear a whole bunch of that beer whiz on both sides of each roll—4 tablespoons per sandwich should do it. Lay down some onions on one side of the roll and some cherry pepper slices on the other. Place each roll on top of a big-ass sheet of foil. This is foreshadowing. Chekhov's gun and all that.

8 When the oil's smoking, drop in about half a pound of beef, which is enough for one sando. Dust the meat with salt as soon as it hits the pan. Let it sear for about a minute on one side—you want a little bit of char—then sauté it around to finish cooking.

9 Using tongs, transfer the hot meat (lol, hot meat) directly into a roll—really smash it in there—then fold the foil around the sandwich so no air can escape. The meat is going to steam the bread and re-melt the cheese to molten status. It's a fucking thermodynamic Christmas miracle. Make the remaining sandwiches. You won't need to add more oil because enough beef fat should be rendered in the pan from the previous batch. Wait at least 3 minutes before eating.

CAP'N DRUNK PANCAKES

with Malt Glaze

MAKES 8 MEDIUM PANCAKES,
ABOUT 3 SERVINGS

Pancakes

4 cups nondescriptly flavored golden square breakfast cereal whose mascot holds military rank

1 cup flour

1½ teaspoons baking powder

½ teaspoon baking soda

½ teaspoon salt

1 can light beer

1 cup whole milk

1 egg

2 tablespoons butter, melted; plus more for cooking the pancakes

Glaze

2 tablespoons whole milk

1 tablespoon butter

1 cup powdered sugar

2 tablespoons malted milk powder (if you can't find malt powder, use powdered milk; it will at least give you an extra dose of funk in there)

This recipe employs a technique—I'm pretty sure it's a classical French pastry thing—where you sub out stupid boring white flour for sugary and nostalgic breakfast cereal. I might have learned about it on *Chef's Table*. There was Beethoven playing in the background (or whatever), and then some dude in a white hat dusts a cutting board with Fruity Pebbles in a super slo-mo shot. Can't remember which episode though. I'll get back to you on that. The technique doesn't only apply to pancakes, either. You can add cereal crumbs to cookie dough or cake batter, or basically any batter or dough that doesn't rely on gluten development like donuts or pizza do. I suggest you do it, and after you eat these pancakes, you'll see why.

---

1 For the pancakes: Put the breakfast cereal and flour in a food processor or blender and let it run on high until the cereal is properly dusted up. (Or empty it into a large Ziploc bag and bash it repeatedly with a blunt object—like a can of beans or a brick.) Empty that into a large mixing bowl and add the baking powder, baking soda, and salt.

2 In a separate mixing bowl, combine the beer, milk, egg, and melted butter and whisk together.

3 Slowly pour your wet ingredients into your dry ingredients and whisk together.

4 Heat about a teaspoon of butter in a large nonstick sauté pan over medium heat. Or one of those big electric griddles...Man, I should get one of those. They seem useful. But where would I even put it, you know?

5 When the butter is fully melted, pour in about a ½ cup of your pancake batter and swirl the pan a little bit so the batter disperses evenly. Fit as many pancakes as you can into the pan without the edges touching. Or you can go one at a time and spend all day at the stove. Either way.

6 When bubbles start to form on top of the pancake (or when you smell it burning, I don't know), after about 3 minutes, flip the pancake and cook for another 2 on the other side, until the batter is cooked through and there's some good browning on the outsides. Repeat until all the batter is used. To keep the pancakes warm until serving, wrap them together in tin foil. It will insulate the heat and get some good steam action going, which will keep them tender and moist.

7 To make the glaze: Heat a small saucepot on medium-low heat, and add the milk and butter. When the butter melts, whisk in the powdered sugar and malt powder. Whisk over the heat for 15 seconds, then turn off the heat.

8 Stack those cakes at least three-high on a plate, pour a bunch of glaze over the top, then garnish with some extra crushed-up breakfast cereal that for sure doesn't rhyme with "Faptain Brunch."

CAP'N DRUNK
PANCAKES WITH
MALT GLAZE, *page 15*

BREW-NUT CARAMEL SUNDAE

MAKES 4 SUNDAES

1½ cups sugar
1 can light beer
1 stick (8 tablespoons) butter
1 cup roasted salted peanuts
1 pint vanilla ice cream
Marshmallow fluff

Beer and ice cream go together like lamb and tuna fish. Or in your country, maybe spaghetti and meatball. Bonus points if you get the reference.

Even though beer and ice cream is a generally good thing, I don't think people are necessarily doing it right. Seems like every wannabe cool restaurant has to have an obligatory beer float somewhere on the menu, but beer floats suck. Can you imagine if a server just walked around with a gravy boat of heavy cream and poured it into your beer? Because that's exactly what a beer float is.

I want the essence and funk of beer with the pure sweet sugary goodness of ice cream, and I don't want either element to negatively affect the other. That's where beer caramel comes into play. Thanks to all the butter, it still has the consistency of a cream-heavy caramel, plus all the beer stank (I use that term endearingly) you could ask for.

1 Spread the sugar out in an even layer in a large saucepan (you'll need that room later) and place on medium-high heat.

2 While the sugar is melting, add the beer and butter to a medium saucepan and crank the heat to high. Stir the mixture until the butter is melted, then drop it to low heat and let it hang.

3 OK cool, back to that pan full of sugar. You'll see it start to melt into brown stuff—also known, to some, as caramel—at the edges. Continuously whisk the caramel until all the lumps disappear and it turns a deep amber, about 8 minutes. Don't need to go too aggressive on burning it.

4 Turn the caramel burner to low. Take your buttery beer juice and slowly whisk it into the caramel. The mixture is going to foam up a bunch, so watch your face. When all the liquid is incorporated, turn the heat back to medium, cook for another 30 seconds, then turn the heat off. Add the peanuts. That's it. Let the mixture come to just above room temp before serving.

5 Use a scoop to scoop a scoop of ice cream into a bowl. Or maybe a champagne coupe. I don't know. Do something adorable. Top it with a hefty ladling of your brew-nut caramel, then a scoop of marshmallow fluff.

BEER-POACHED BRATWURST PARTY SUB

MAKES 1 BIG-ASS SANDWICH, SERVING 4, AT LEAST

4 cans light beer

4 cloves garlic, crushed

4 chilies de arbol

2 shallots, peeled and sliced in half lengthwise

2 tablespoons whole mustard seeds

1 tablespoon whole black peppercorns

1 tablespoon whole coriander seeds

8 fatty pork brats

2 tablespoons vegetable oil

1 large loaf French bread

1 (32-ounce) jar sauerkraut

3 tablespoons yellow mustard

3 tablespoons mayonnaise

1½ tablespoons Sriracha

8 slices Swiss cheese

The first time I made a bratwurst party sub—and it sure as hell won't be the last—I live streamed it on the once-relevant social media application Periscope. My roommates Nick and Ryan and I had just gotten back from track practice, and we were looking to binge-eat something fierce.

We got a loaf of French bread, sliced it open, dressed it with a bunch of mustard and kraut and pickles and cheese, and started searing off some brats. It was a hot summer day, and we were all sticky from practice, so, naturally, we had taken our shirts off. You know, as one does when one's frying pork products.

Our Periscope live stream was titled #SAUSAGEFEST2015, on account of that we were making several sausages and it was the year of our lord 2015. We tucked the sausages into the bread, and, rather than slicing the sandwich into thirds, we were so hungry that we just took turns shoving it into our faces.

We noticed that our view count was steadily growing. We reached 100, then 200, then 300…and still climbing. Some of the comments were sexually explicit. Some of the comments were instructing us to do things to each other with the promise of monetary compensation.

That's when we took a step back and assessed the situation. We were three 250-plus-pound shirtless men on a live streaming app shoving sausages into our faces and physically wrestling over a sandwich with an event titled #SAUSAGEFEST2015. We closed out our stream and ate the rest of the sandwich in silence. I still wonder what would have happened if I had pursued gay fetish porn instead. What if…

1 In a large stockpot, combine the beer, garlic, chilies, shallots, mustard seeds, peppercorns, and coriander and slam the burner on high. Bring the mixture to a boil and let cook down for about 10 minutes, until it's reduced by half.

2 Toss in the sausages, making sure they're all submerged. Bring the pot to a boil again and cook for about 10 minutes, until the brats are all cooked through. Don't turn off the heat though, you'll need it again later.

3 Remove the sausages with tongs and let dry on some paper towels. Heat the oil in a large sauté pan on high heat. When the oil moves freely around the pan, sear off your brats, working in batches of four at a time. You're really just trying to get some color on the sausages because boiled sausages look like dicks, and, even though all the best foods look like dicks, we—as a society—still try to remove ourselves from that.

4 When the sausages are nice and browned, throw them back into the poaching liquid and continue to simmer for 5 minutes.

5 Slice the loaf of French bread in half, then throw it under a hot broiler, cut-side up, for a minute to get some char on it. You want a crusty protection layer so the meat juices don't immediately fuck up the structural integrity of your sandwich.

6 Heat up the sauerkraut. Just microwave it, I guess. Who am I to say though, really?

7 Whisk together the mustard, mayo, and Sriracha (the combo works, I swear), then splash it on both sides of the bread. On the bottom layer, shingle all the cheese, then top it with all your sausages coming straight from the hot poaching liquid, then blanket the whole thing in more steaming hot sauerkraut than you think you need. About half the jar should do.

8 For the death blow, strain your poaching liquid, which should now be pleasantly infused with fragrant sausage fat, into a bowl. Pour about a cup of that liquid (more if you nasty) on top of the sauerkraut and let it trickle through the rest of the sandwich.

9 **This step seems stupid, but it's not:** Put the top part of the bread on top of the sandwich, then, being very careful not to fuck it up, flip it over and let it rest upside down for 3 minutes. This is going to reverse the flow of juices and evenly distribute them.

10 Slice your bread loaf monstrosity into four equal parts. Shit... maybe more than four. Sometimes I literally forget how much reasonable people eat. Whatever, you'll figure it out. If there's leftover poaching liquid, use it as au jus and French-dip the fuck out of it.

The easiest game is
called Drink the Beer.
The rules are as follows:
(1) Drink the beer. It's
great because it's
inclusive and
everybody wins.

GRILLED-PINEAPPLE BEERGRIA

SERVES 5 TO 15,

depending on how well you and your friends can hold your light beer

3 fresh pineapples

10 limes

10 lemons

5 oranges

2 cups pomegranate molasses (may need to buy 2 bottles)

30-pack light beer

Ahhh, the story of beergria is as old as time itself. Or as old as 2012, but whatever. We were having a birthday party for our dear friend Hannah, and Hannah always had the most lit parties. One of Hannah's friends volunteered as tribute to get three bags of pink wine, then I was going to slice up a bunch of citrus fruit, and we were going to dump it into a giant bucket and get shitty off pink sangria.

Our alcohol liaison flaked, so we were left alcohol-less, on Hannah's birthday—the most holy of days—with all the liquor stores within walking distance closed. But, just like the Maccabees' lantern burned bright for eight days instead of one, so too did we get drunk. We found an emergency 30-pack of Busch Light stashed in our alley. Not wanting to let some perfectly good citrus fruit go to waste, we poured all the beers into the bucket. But the dueling aromas of warm piss and fresh citrus made it undrinkable. I searched my pantry for anything that might make it palatable and stumbled upon a bottle of pomegranate molasses. We dumped it into our bucket, stirred it up, and the result was nothing short of a miracle. A Chanukah miracle. Seriously though, the acid in the pomegranate molasses totally makes it.

1 Light a grill on high heat. Remove the skin from the pineapples, trim off the tops and bottoms, then slice into 1-inch-thick rounds. Don't worry about coring them. When the grill is screaming hot, sear off the pineapple rounds for about 2 minutes on each side, until you get a good amount of char on there. Take them off the grill and reserve for later.

2 Get yourself a big-ass bucket. Like a really big bucket. Doesn't even have to be a food bucket, just get one from a hardware store. Trim the ends off the limes, lemons, and oranges and slice those into rounds, then throw them into the bucket.

3 Pour the pomegranate molasses all over the fruit, then use some sort of stick to muddle it together a bit. You want some of the fruit juice to interact with the pomegranate molasses and create a citrusy-sweet-flavor sludge.

4 Add your grilled pineapple on top, then pour over as much of the 30-rack as will fit in the bucket. You probably can't fit all the beers in there, so, when the liquid level gets low in the bucket, just pour more beers over the top. Use that stick you have to mix the beer with the fruit, then scoop straight from the bucket with a red cup. Boom. Beergria.

Drunk MUNCHIES

THE TWO TYPES

of Drunk Cooking

▶ To understand the dichotomy of deliberate drunk cooking versus spontaneous drunk cooking, you must first understand art history.

In the mid-1800s, the Impressionists broke from traditional paint-mixing techniques and codified brushstrokes to more authentically capture a moment in time. Small and erratic flicks of color create emotional depth and a sense of movement that forces your eye to navigate the canvas so quickly you're afraid the painting will disappear if you blink. Impressionism changed the way we consume an image. It is not ours to stare at, but to experience, if for but an instant.

Soon thereafter, the Expressionists took the same energy and emotion found in Impressionism and focused it inwards, transforming their own thoughts and feelings into the subject of the painting. The results were often dreamlike and distorted, any realistic element skewed through the filter of the mind. Figures often appeared dark and grotesque, more like creatures of a morbid fantasy than anything seen in nature. Because they were.

Deliberate drunk cooking—making a conscious decision to consume alcohol before setting fire to food—is like Impressionism. You're going into the project with a general plan and a basic understanding of technique, even though you know there will be flourishes and embellishments along the way, both intended and unintended.

You can predict the general shape of the final product, and you may even have an idea of what it's going to taste like, but the dish is ultimately process-dependent, its mysteries only revealed through the journey of intoxication.

Like Monet's water lilies, the form is ephemeral. What was once a bread bowl filled with meatballs and cheese, deluged in garnet and ivory, is now aflame. Moments in the broiler left uncaptured while thumbs twiddled Xbox joysticks and ass smothered couch. You might have smoked a little weed too and totally forgot that you were cooking. Promises unfulfilled.

The wet dishtowel you're using to bludgeon the fire is as much a part of the dish as garlic or Parmesan. Action suspended in the consumable. Your work borders on edible; if you just scrape the burnt parts off the bread and do your best to remove the cat hair in the sauce, you can probably save a third of it. There is a lot of cat hair.

Spontaneous drunk cooking—getting super fucked up and coming home to find out there's no food and also being too drunk to go back out in public, so whatever, man, let's get weird with some Doritos and a box of Rice-A-Roni—is like Expressionism.

There's an autonomic element to your cooking that you can't control. Your emotions flood the plate. You might think you're pouring the packet of mac and cheese seasoning into the pot, but actually you dumped it directly onto the stove because your astigmatism gets really bad when you drink and depth perception has never been a strong suit and holy shit are the lights just not on?

You are left with plain noodles. The gift of a blank canvas. Purity of the soul. Perhaps your macaroni will be enrobed in mayonnaise because your mind perceives mayo to be indistinguishable from cheese.

Sriracha lashes starch. The rooster: totem of masculinity, of passion, of rage and heat and flame; and also you want your shit to be orange because you know that mac and cheese is orange so this will probably work.

The pot is alive. Noodles quake and tremble, astringent hot sauce fumes rise, mayo latches onto the pot in a crusty show of resistance that a wooden spoon refuses to disturb. Plastic gnarls and twists as it melts into the side of the pot, the macaroni packaging a scorched and crumpled version of what used to be.

Just as Jackson Pollock left cigarette butts in his paintings, you will leave the bag fused to the pot. And also, like, how do you even clean that? Do you have to remelt the plastic or is that just going to make it worse? Should I just throw the pot away?

Yeah, so most of these recipes are things I've deliberately gotten drunk and cooked. Spontaneous drunk cooking gets really messy, and the end result is generally terrible and not something you ever want to write down.

There have been a few hits over the years: BBQ beef spaghetti with leftover pancake breadcrumbs made a surprising amount of sense. But for every one of those, you get an orange chicken and brie calzone with sweet-and-sour marinara. Fuck. That was such a bad decision.

A VERY DRUNK

BIRTHDAY CAKE
Tradition

Different friend groups have different ways of honoring birthdays. Some will pool their money together to buy the special person a very special gift or a plane ticket somewhere or send them on an unwitting scavenger hunt (apparently that's a thing that people do) or take them to some stupid club or something.

We didn't do any of that. We would throw an obligatory party, sure, but that could have been on any weekend. There was one tradition that we did adhere to though: We'd all get super fucked up and bake a super grotesque, monstrous, often highly conceptualized birthday cake.

The first year we all lived together in the Santa Barbara duplex, Dave's birthday was first on the calendar. I asked him what kind of cake he liked, because I wanted to bake a big-ass cake and then also eat that big-ass cake. But Dave doesn't like cake. Like, at all, apparently. Dave likes grasshopper pie (mint chocolate ice cream in a chocolate crust), and chocolate chip cookies, and bacon. So I took that into consideration.

DAVE'S CAKE

Two frozen grasshopper pies sandwiched between 3 white sponge cakes with blackberries and chocolate chip cookies blended into the batter, all slathered in maple bacon buttercream and finished with a fresh mango and rum glaze.

You may have noticed that none of those ingredients seem to go together. That is a very astute observation—this cake was largely inedible, and also the grasshopper pies started melting almost immediately because I forgot to let the cakes adequately cool. It also weighed, somehow, more than 20 pounds. We ended up having a food fight with it on the front lawn because it was truly disgusting. But this was just the first.

MARCUS'S CAKE

A 12-pack of Dos Equis with the top layer of cardboard sliced off and 6 interior beers removed was filled with a fully garnished beef nacho platter, then topped with a single layer of chocolate sheet cake, and the whole thing—box and all—was covered in a layer of white frosting. The words Happy Beerthday Marcus *were inscribed on the top in black decorative icing, and a single bottle of Dos Equis was jammed into the cake.*

This was it. This was my magnum opus. I don't know that I'll ever do anything this awesome again in my life. Dude, we hid a 12-pack of beer inside a cake, and then we hid a fucking nacho platter inside a 12-pack of beer. Who does that? No, seriously, I'm asking because if you know someone who does in fact do that, I would like to meet them. Marcus loves beer and nachos more than anyone I've ever known, and I wish you could have been at the party that day to see the look on his face when he sliced into that cake and it immediately gave way and revealed a secret stash of beer. Or when he tried to grab the secret stash of beer only to reveal a hidden nacho cave.

EMIL'S CAKE

Two quiches stacked on top of each other using 6 total pie crusts and filled with 2 dozen eggs, 64 ounces of half-and-half, 5 cans of corned beef hash, 12 McDoubles, 2 large McDonald's fries, 24 mozzarella strips, 3 pounds of Dino nuggets, 3 pounds of bacon, and 40 Totino's pizza rolls, then slathered in a Spam-and-bacon-fat cream gravy and garnished with an entire family-sized bag of crushed jalapeño-flavored kettle-cooked potato chips. We wrote "Happy Birthday" in Sriracha, and then, using the leftover Dino nuggets, someone drew a reenactment of the extinction of the dinosaurs directly on the table with ketchup.

Marcus's cake may have been my architectural masterpiece, but **Emil's cake was for sure my shock-and-awe masterpiece.** No one else wanted to throw in cash because my idea was so goddamned over-the-top and stupid, so I footed the entire $200 bill myself. It was worth every penny. If anyone knows anything about Emil, it's that he eats shitty convenience foods like it's no one's business, and I wasn't going to let my muse get away from me. This was my dream project, and I think it got knocked out of the fucking park. The Cheeseburger Pudding recipe on page 34 was actually inspired by Emil's monstrous quiche cake. So if you want to taste a little slice of Emil, have at it.

You've probably seen the words *cheeseburger* and *pudding* before. But you probably haven't seen them listed in succession, and you definitely haven't seen them listed in succession on purpose. That's because it's a stupid idea. When you're working with a fully pre-raided fridge and you're too drunk to remember the delivery number for trash pizza, sometimes you gotta make do with a bunch of eggs, cheese, and frozen burgers. It's a metaphor for life, really. I don't know for what, specifically, but you know. It's probably true. And if the phrase "cheeseburger pudding" weirds you out too much, just think of it as a crustless cheeseburger quiche. See? That's way more normal, bordering on fancy. I'd pay $16.99 for a slice of crustless cheeseburger quiche with a mixed baby greens salad on the side, easy.

CHEESEBURGER
PUDDING

SERVES 6

1 eight-pack microwavable hamburgers (preferably White Castle cheeseburger sliders)

1 (12-ounce) package shredded sharp cheddar cheese (or the equivalent in whatever the fuck cheese you want)

1 cup milk or cream or whatever

8 eggs

1 teaspoon salt

½ teaspoon black pepper

Ketchup, for drizzling

1 Get ready, man, because this recipe is heavy.

2 No, really, this is some complicated, classical French technique shit.

3 Alright, if you're still down, preheat the oven to 400°F, grease a deep casserole, and let's do it.

4 Microwave those burgers according to the directions on the package. When sufficiently microwaved, chop them into roughly 1-inch-square pieces. Throw into the casserole.

5 Whisk together all the other shit. Except the ketchup. The ketchup is sacred. Don't involve ketchup in this mess right now. Pour it over the cheeseburgers and gently mix by hand, being tender and careful not to just completely mash all the shit into one homogeneous slop mush.

6 Bake it for 30 minutes, until golden brown and no moisture remains. Take it out without burning yourself.

7 Use a butter knife to get the edges unstuck from the casserole dish and flip the whole thing over. If all has gone well, your cheeseburger pudding will have come out in perfect loaf form.

8 Cut yourself a thick slice of that abomination of food, drizzle some ketchup on it, preferably garnish it with something green, and then fall asleep before you eat it, because you've had a long night, bud.

RAVIOLI TRASH PIZZA

SERVES BETWEEN 0 AND 4 PEOPLE

1 family-sized frozen pizza

1 family-sized can ravioli

Optional Toppings

4 ounces imported mozzarella di bufala

Leaves of basil, for garnish

2 ounces quality prosciutto di parma

Olive oil, for drizzling

This recipe is pure trash. I mean, this is some straight dirtbag-type shit. Like this is the pre-Bawitdaba-era Kid Rock of recipes. Part of me wants to apologize for it, but, since I've never apologized for anything I've done while drunk (that's not true, I'm constantly apologizing), I'm not going to start now. It would be in bad form. And this totally made sense at the time. I had a frozen pizza—well, my roommate had a frozen pizza, but, again, drunk—and frozen pizzas are always undersauced and shitty, so I dumped a can of (also my roommate's) trash ravioli on it.

Does it taste good? The short answer is no, not if you're sober. It tastes like trash pizza topped with trash ravioli because it's a trash pizza topped with trash ravioli. How much you enjoy this chimeric trash monster is directly correlated to how much you've had to drink, so think of it as a choose-your-own-adventure recipe.

1 Preheat your oven to 400°F, then unwrap the frozen trash pizza and open the can of trash ravioli. Dump the ravioli onto the pizza.

2 If you're using the optional mozzarella di bufala—and I suggest you do because I think it's hilarious—slice it into rounds and arrange them evenly across the trash pizza.

3 Put it in the oven for, who knows, 20 minutes? When you smell it burning, take it out.

4 If you're not using the other optional garnishes—come *onnn,* you should really do it; indulge me for one goddamned second—you can slice it and eat right away. If you are using the optional garnishes—oh my God, finally, thank you!—sprinkle some basil leaves on there and lovingly lay a few sheets of prosciutto down. Drizzle some olive oil over the top. Maybe some fresh shaved Reggiano. Or just throw the whole thing in the trash. Your choice.

BUFFALO
FRIED RICE

SERVES 1

2 tablespoons vegetable oil

1 cup cooked white rice
(preferably Jackie's)

1 egg

¼ cup buffalo sauce

2 tablespoons minced celery

¼ cup blue cheese dressing

2 tablespoons minced scallions

(If you have some precooked
chicken breast lying around,
toss that in too, but don't strain
yourself.)

All you really need from your drunk food is a vehicle, right? You just need a flavor conduit, something to prevent you from, say, drinking a bottle of buffalo sauce and rubbing blue cheese crumbles into your gums just so you can get on that sweet, sweet flavor high, right? Right. It almost doesn't even matter what it is. It could be a pile of chips; it could be a bucket of ramen; it could be some stale school lunch–issue white bread. Hell, it could even be the leftover rice that your Taiwanese roommate Jackie would leave in the rice cooker all day but the rice cooker is covered so it's totally safe or at least that's what you tell yourself. Fucking bingo.

Jackie's leftover rice was more than just stale mushy carbs when you stumbled home drunk, it was stale mushy opportunity. You could go anywhere with this—Buffalo fried rice, BBQ fried rice, marinara fried rice, regular-ass soy sauce fried rice. Basically any bottle of non-expired sauce you have in the fridge can make you some mediocre-but-necessary fried rice when treated with proper technique.

---

1 Put the vegetable oil in a large heavy-bottomed sauté pan (you probably don't have a wok, right?) and heat the fuck out of it. Just really crank it to high and let it run for at least 3 minutes. When the oil is smoking, add your cooked rice and use a spatula to sauté for about 2 minutes, keeping it moving around the pan. If you have spare chicken lying around, now's the time to throw it in.

2 Move the rice to one side of the pan, then crack the egg in the other side. Mix the egg around with a spatula until it starts to form curds, then incorporate it into the rice and continue to sauté.

3 Add the buffalo sauce. It's gonna fume up and it's going to sting your eyes and nostrils and you're going to have a genuinely bad time, but nothing good comes without pain and sacrifice. Tom Colicchio said that. Maybe. Stir the sauce in and continue to sauté for an additional 30 seconds, until the buffalo goodness starts to really be absorbed by the rice.

4 Turn off the heat, add the celery, and stir it up. Put it in a bowl, drizzle some blue cheese dressing over the top, and throw on some scallions for color. Being shithoused is no excuse for sloppy presentation.

One day, I was intoxicated and wanted nachos, as intoxicated people are often wont to want. I came home and found a big-ass bag of tortilla chips, except the three-pound block of cheddar that my roommate Marcus would buy every week (he had a problem) was down to a nub. Just a snack nub too. Sucks. So I improvised. I found some boxed macaroni and cheese and figured that if I followed the instructions on the box and omitted the pasta, it would create a perfect nacho cheese sauce.

That was dumb. I am dumb. Turns out, all that starch from the pasta is really what makes the orange goo water thicken. The lessons life teaches you, man. So I boiled the macaroni, stirred it into the sauce, and shamelessly dumped the whole thing on a bed of chips. Me and Tom Colicchio are one and the same, really.

MAC 'N' CHEESE NACHOS

SERVES 1

(Let's be real—if you're drunk enough to make this recipe, you're also drunk enough to eat an entire tray of it.)

1 big-ass bag tortilla chips

1 big-ass box macaroni and cheese

1 jar pickled jalapeños

Sriracha and sour cream, for garnish

1 Get yourself some sort of trough. When I make drunk nachos, my general game plan is to use a giant baking sheet for a plate. I'd advise you to do the same. Unless you have an actual pig trough, because that would be rad. Do that. Spread out that whole bag of chips evenly onto your trough.

2 Make the macaroni and cheese according to the box. Like, I can't tell you how to do it any better than they can. They probably tell you to boil noodles, then put a bunch of butter and milk in a pan, then stir in an orange powder, then mash everything together. Do that, then stir in a tablespoon of pickled jalapeño liquid, because it will make your mac and cheese taste like ballpark nachos. I was way too proud of myself for doing that at the time this recipe was conceived.

3 I guess you should pour all that mac and cheese onto all those chips, because, they're both right in front of you. It would be stupid not to. **PRO TIP:** Throw a fucking Sriracha squiggle on there. Immediately improves the aesthetic quality of whatever you're eating. Just a bunch of arbitrary Sriracha lines. Then drop some jalapeño rings, and throw a dollop of sour cream on there if you nasty.

MAC 'N' CHEESE NACHOS,
page 39

I'm no nutritionist—if you thought I was, I apologize for misleading you—but this seems like a pretty balanced meal. Think about it: You have all that protein from the eggs, you have carbs from the noodles, and you have like six days' worth of sodium. It's perfect. I'm willing to call it a superfood if you are. Also, for how amazingly nutritious it is, it's absurdly cheap. Like if you're out there throwing bills and getting blotto all night and want to come home to some drunk food that won't break the bank, the ramelette is the right way to go. It's also infinitely customizable: You can add more ramen to your ramelette, or more eggs, or even more seasoning, provided you have another seasoning packet! Am I just overly psyched about it to compensate for this being, objectively, the saddest recipe of all time? Maybe! OK, let's get to it!

RAMELETTE

SERVES 1

1 package instant ramen (chicken and shrimp flavors work best)

4 eggs

Nonstick cooking spray

Condiments of choice

1   Fill a medium saucepot halfway with water, then bring it to a boil. Drop the ramen noodles in. Do not—I REPEAT, DO FUCKING NOT—empty the seasoning packet into the noodles. That has a very special purpose that you will find out about soon. Cook the noodles for 3 minutes and drain.

2   That soon time is now! Crack all of the eggs into a large mixing bowl and whisk them together along with the seasoning from the packet.

3   Lather up a large sauté pan with nonstick cooking spray, then heat it on medium.

4   When the pan is hot, after 2 or 3 minutes, add your egg mixture. Then dump in all your drained ramen noodles and gently press them into the raw egg mixture. Cover the pan with something, even if it's just foil, to help cook the eggs faster. Don't worry about overcooking your eggs here, you really want to shoot for al dente.

5   After about 6 minutes, when the bottom of the ramelette is fully set (lift up an edge to check), flip it over to the other side. Cook for an additional 4 minutes, or until cooked all the way through.

6   Slide your ramelette out onto a plate, then proceed to throw various condiments at it until it tastes better. These may include, but are not limited to: ketchup, Sriracha, a whole jar of Pace salsa, or a thwap of Greek yogurt if you're trying to be healthy.

MEATBALL
BREAD
BOWLS

1 pound ground beef

1 egg

½ cup grated Parmesan cheese

¼ cup chopped parsley

1 cup breadcrumbs

½ teaspoon red chili flakes

1 teaspoon salt

¼ teaspoon black pepper

¼ cup whole milk

Vegetable oil, for drizzling

2 large sourdough boules (circle loaves)

1 big-ass jar marinara sauce

1 big-ass jar Alfredo sauce

1 cup shredded mozzarella

See, this is why I don't plan things. Every time you try and deliberately make something happen, shit hits the fan. You have to let things come naturally, to let the energy flow as nature intended and not force the issue. A buddy and I made plans—like we texted and set a date and everything—to get fucked up and cook something real stupid and indulgent and depraved. So we did. We came up with the plan for a meatball-sandwich-type thing but served in a big-ass hollowed-out sourdough bread bowl.

Things went great. At first. We drank a bunch of dark liquor, I made the meatballs, he hollowed out the bread, we dumped in the sauce and blanketed the whole thing with the salty bagged mozzarella that makes everything taste like Domino's pizza and threw it under the broiler. Then we sat. We were going to play video games for five minutes while our monstrosity finished cooking. I destroyed him in a game of FIFA because I'm a natural-born winner, and then I destroyed him again because I show no mercy.

Then the smoke alarm went off. The view through the oven door was a blanket of orange. As it turns out, when there's an open flame near bread and greasy cheese for long enough, it will start a fire. It did. They don't teach you that in Scouts. We took the flaming bread bowls out of the oven and started slapping at them with a wet dishtowel until we no longer thought we were going to die. We threw them out and went to Taco Bell. Still a rock-solid concept though, as long as you don't get distracted by whipping some ass in FIFA.

1   Preheat your oven to 400°F. Grease a baking sheet.

2   Use your hands to mix together the ground beef, egg, Parmesan, parsley, breadcrumbs, chili flakes, salt, black pepper, and milk.

3   Form your meat mixture into 1-inch spheres, then plop them down onto the greased-up baking sheet, making sure there's space in between each of the balls. Don't let the balls touch. Never let the balls touch. Drizzle each with some vegetable oil and throw in the 400-degree oven for 25 to 30 minutes, until they are nice and brown and won't give you E. coli.

4   Cut a circle in the top of the sourdough boules and use your hands to scrape out the insides until you're left with two nice bowls, ready to be filled with shit. Eat the bread insides.

5   Dump your meatballs into the boules until they almost reach the opening and then pour the jarred pasta sauces over the top. You can mix the sauces together to form a sort of mock vodka sauce, but I like to keep them separate so I can sort of mix and match bites of red and white.

6   When the sauce is filled almost to the brim, pack the cheese in the openings to seal it. Throw it all in the 400-degree oven for 10 minutes so it gets all nice and melty and toasty.

7   Don't burn your fucking house down.

GRILLED STUFFED S'MORES BURRITOS

SERVES 2

2 large flour tortillas

½ cup milk chocolate chips

8 large marshmallows; or a bunch of the tiny ones

2 large graham cracker sheets (the kind where it has four separate tiny crackers cut out in perforations)

One of my life's biggest accomplishments is blacking out and making a funnel cake. I don't remember making it per se—which is scary because there's a lot of hot oil involved in funnel cakes—but through some *Memento*-style sleuthing I figured it out. And by *Memento*-style sleuthing, I mean I woke up and found a funnel that I use for my car covered in batter, a saucepot full of used canola oil, and grease splatters all over my linoleum floor. I vaguely remember eating the funnel cake, but only because I remember how stoked I was that I bought honey the night before, because I literally soaked the entire thing in honey. I mean, it was floating in a pool of honey and I ate it with my hands and I woke up sticky. So, so sticky.

These s'mores burritos have nothing to do with that blacked-out funnel cake story; I just thought it was funny, and since I don't remember what I did to make the funnel cake, you'll have to settle for this. That's my bad.

1 Heat a large sauté pan on high heat. When it's super-hot but not smoking, griddle off one tortilla for 15 seconds on each side, just so it's pliable enough to work with. Repeat with the other tortilla because I assume you're not a selfish dickbag and you're making some for your friends. Set aside the tortillas, but leave the pan on medium heat. You'll see why later! Stay tuned!

2 Lay down half of the chocolate chips on one tortilla, then 4 marshmallows running right down the center. Keep everything in the middle; by the way, you need to keep the edges clear so you can fold it all up. Work smart, not hard or whatever.

3 Take one graham cracker sheet and crush it with your hands. Yeah, really be a man about it. Get some aggression out. Act like that graham cracker is your stepdad who wouldn't let you play Xbox after 8 p.m. Dump the crushed graham onto the marshmallows, then fold the burrito up. Repeat to make another burrito.

4 Remember when I said you'd be using that pan again? I wasn't lying! You're about to use it!

5 The pan should be pretty searing-hot by now. Place the crease-side of each burrito down on the surface, then gently press them down. Searing off the crease will create some steam between tortilla layers, helping them naturally fuse together and creating a tighter seal. Sear for about 30 seconds, until the tortilla gets some brownish color on it, then turn each burrito 90 degrees and sear for 30 seconds on each side. This will also help the chocolate and mallows get all melty. Remove from the pan.

6 If you put a burrito in your mouth immediately without waiting, you're going to seriously fuck your day up. Like real bad. But who am I to tell you what to do?

FOOD IN

Dirt

THE TAO of Tom Colicchio

▶ My roommate Marcus and I once watched Tom Colicchio say a bunch of words on a stage. We even paid money to see him do it, which is a big deal, because money can buy a lot of things, and I like things.

His speech started at 7:30 p.m. in one of the main lecture halls at UC Santa Barbara (woooo, Gauchos rule!), and I had a class across campus that ended at 8, so I politely asked the TA if I could bounce early because it's not often that you get to be near one of your heroes, let alone watch him talk at you.

My TA said no and I told him I was going to do it anyways. He asked me if I cared about my grade. I laughed uncontrollably and walked out.

I met Marcus outside the theater. He was wearing a casual Levi's button-down shirt and some dark Levi's jeans because he worked at the Levi's store downtown and got a discount. I was wearing a sweat-stained maroon T-shirt with a cartoon pig on it, and I was covered in lifting chalk and dried blood because I'd just finished track practice and I also have very little self-respect.

We were the only college students there, the only people under 40 years old, and the only people not rocking blazers, heels, and the shit-eating-smug-motherfucker-grin that comes with being a wealthy Santa Barbara socialite. Everyone stared at us like we were assholes because we were, indeed, assholes. But whatever, we were here for one reason only: to pay homage to the *Top Chef* god.

People like to have mantras—things they can repeat over and over and over to themselves *ad nauseam* as some sort of universal truth that's easily digestible and makes them feel in control. It's useful as fuck; you should grab a mantra. For most people, it's something a family member once said, or maybe a mentor, or most likely it's just some shit they heard in a movie or saw on a poster.

My mantra came from Tom Colicchio that day. He was talking about growing up working at ballpark concession stands every summer and how, even though it was hot and grueling, that was the most comfortable he ever felt. He talked about working in restaurant kitchens as a teen. An executive chef once made him clean and peel 50 pounds of shrimp and he didn't leave the kitchen until 2 a.m. and that's when he learned what it truly meant to grind.

Colicchio told the crowd that he was a promising high school swimmer and he was offered a college scholarship. I tried googling his times but found nothing because, duh, the fucking Internet wasn't around back then. So who knows.

The point is, he came to the same crossroads that I came to: You love the fuck out of sports, and you love the fuck out of food, but you have to choose one because life is shitty and unfair.

And then
I screamed, "I LOVE
YOU, TOM, YOU
LIFE-AFFIRMING
SILVER-FOX
MOTHERFUCKER . . ."

Tom chose food. He kept working in restaurants through high school, and he told the crowd he knew the kitchen life was for him the day he hooked up with a waitress in the back of a Volkswagen in the restaurant parking lot. Whether it happened or not, it's a good story. And he told us that we were the first group of people he ever told it to.

I chose sports. I took a track-and-field scholarship to UCSB because at the time I knew how to throw heavy metal objects better than I knew how to cook. And that freaked me out. Why didn't I do what Tom did?

He had an open Q&A session afterwards and I raised my hand and he pointed at me: "What would've happened if you took that swimming scholarship?"

"Ha! Oh shit, who knows?" That wasn't the inspiring part of his answer. That was just something mildly self-deprecating and vulgar and endearingly Tom Colicchio-esque. Then he said, "No matter what path you choose in life, your passions have a habit of rising to the top."

And then I screamed, "I LOVE YOU, TOM, YOU LIFE-AFFIRMING SILVER-FOX MOTHERFUCKER," and ran up onstage to try and hug him before getting Tased by security.

That last part didn't happen, but all the other stuff did.

I've repeated that mantra over and over and over in my head—*Passion rises to the top.* That Colicchio's passion involves dry-aged steaks and potato *dauphinoise,* and mine involves getting drunk and deep-frying snack foods is beside the point. Passion rises to the top.

He talked about other things too. Other inspiring things, because he's the type of person who could say literally anything and be inspiring. Tom Colicchio could be like, "You should wait half an hour after eating before you get in the pool," and you'd be like, "Holy shit, I have to write that down. Did you just make that up?" and it would change your life.

He talked about why recipes are trash and showed us how to create a dish. Random people in the audience spit out names of proteins, vegetables, fruits, and countries—pork belly, Swiss chard, orange, Italy—and Colicchio spun it into half-improv, half-sleight-of-hand magic trick.

"Swiss chard agnolotti with pork belly sugo, orange mostarda, and chicharrón dust." The crowd erupted the way crowds only erupt when someone nails a moderately hard guitar solo or dunks on

Timofey Mozgov. Tom started doing encore performances, spitting people's words back at them in an order that they could taste.

"Smoked and fried Jidori chicken with pickled mustard green stems, pipian verde, and toasted freekeh with cactus pear vinaigrette." More claps.

Even though it sounded like he was just stringing together nouns with more descriptive nouns—which he was—he was also breaking the fourth wall and peeling back the layers of his process. He was revealing the trick. And everyone seemed to think the trick was impressive except for me.

If he can just take plants and meats and colors and add in qualifiers and names of cooking techniques to create a dish, then why couldn't I? I've watched every single episode of *Top Chef* at least twice, I read about food all day, Giada De Laurentiis was basically my surrogate mom growing up—enough information must have stuck inside my head movies to at least be able to regurgitate the right words. And since I know what most foods taste like, either from eating them or hearing very detailed descriptions, I should know which words go together.

I just started doing the Tom Colicchio thing that all the rich white Santa Barbara people were impressed with, and it wasn't that hard. Sometimes I had to google the words that were coming out of my own mouth, which was weird at first, sure, but then I started lying to people and acting like I'd known what burdock root and spigarello were all my life.

Since all of my meals were once based on large cuts of meat, my vegetable-cooking game used to be piss-poor. Then I started to play the Tom Colicchio trick. Throw out a country, a vegetable, an herb, and a fruit, and then try and play the hypothetical bite out in your head.

France. Blue. Maitake mushrooms. Thyme. Lemon. Just slap some descriptors on it, and that nonsensical list of nouns becomes maitake fricassee en croute with thyme jus, blue cheese chantilly, and lemon suprèmes.

And that's how you drop the fucking mic.

DIP'S MOM'S
PAV BHAJI

SERVES 4

4 medium russet potatoes

4 medium Roma tomatoes, stemmed and roughly chopped

2 medium yellow onions, roughly chopped

3 cloves garlic, roughly chopped

1 stick (8 tablespoons) unsalted butter

6 tablespoons pav bhaji masala (find at any Indian market)

1½ teaspoons cayenne

½ head cauliflower, broken into florets

1 cup frozen peas

Salt

½ red onion, thinly sliced

2 tablespoons lemon juice

Warm dinner rolls, for serving

Senior year of high school I stayed at my best friend Dip's house about three times a week. My family moved 30 miles from my school—a two-hour drive with traffic—and I didn't want to transfer, so Dip's family basically adopted me. That's not important. What's important is that his mom is the best goddamned home cook of all time.

Pav bhaji was my favorite dish of hers from jump-street. It's spicy and fragrant and the texture is pure, unrelenting mush, which is something I've come to appreciate on a deep level. Texture is overrated. When she went out of town she would leave just gallons on gallons of food so her now-adult son—and me by proximity—wouldn't live off Taco Bell and frozen pizza.

One day, we decided to throw a party. Because teenagers, am I right? As the party wound down, there were only a handful of fully grown toddlers left, and we were hungry as hell. We scoured the house and found nothing, until Dip pulled out a giant tub of pav bhaji from deep in the freezer. It was like the Donner party stumbling on a freshly roasted buffalo, or whatever the fuck pioneers ate. It was the best bowl of food I'd ever eaten.

1 Fill a large stockpot with at least 6 inches of water and bring it to a boil. Rinse the potatoes and throw them into the water, letting them cook for about 20 minutes, until they can be easily pierced with a fork. Remove the potatoes from the pot, but keep the water boiling. Let the potatoes cool slightly.

2 While the potatoes are boiling away, throw the tomatoes, yellow onions, and garlic in the food processor and let it go on high for 30 seconds.

3 Set a large saucepan on medium-low heat and add the butter. When it melts, pour in your tomato and onion slurry, along with the pav bhaji masala and 1 teaspoon of the cayenne. Simmer for 15 minutes, or until the liquid has reduced by half.

4 Toss the cauliflower and peas into the boiling water used for the potatoes. The water is going to stop boiling when you throw in the veggies, but when it starts boiling again—probably after about a minute—drain the vegetables in a colander and run some cool water over them.

5 When your potatoes are cool enough to work with, remove the skins and give the flesh a quick rough chop. Throw that in the food processor (don't bother cleaning it after the tomatoes and onions, it's all in the same system) and just hit pulse 7 or 8 times. Do not puree. I repeat: DO FUCKING NOT puree the potatoes. You want a little bit of chunk in there. Scoop them chunky potatoes into your pot of simmering tomato goodness.

6 Throw the cauliflower and peas into the food processor (and again disregard cleaning, because fuck that) and hit pulse 7 or 8 times to get the equivalent of a very fine mince. Again, don't puree. If you do, I'm gonna be so mad at you. Stir that into the pot with the tomatoes and potatoes. Simmer on low for about 30 minutes, adding salt to taste along the way. You may need to add a cup of water halfway through to let it keep reducing.

7 While that's simmering, put the thin-sliced red onion in a large bowl and add the lemon juice, along with the remaining ½ teaspoon cayenne. Let that sit for at least 10 minutes.

8 Toast up the regular-ass, white-bread dinner rolls. The "pav" in "pav bhaji" actually comes from the Portuguese word for "bread"—the Portuguese colonized a pretty big region in India and still have a lot of cultural influence in cities like Goa—so the dish is traditionally served with Portuguese rolls. Which are your everyday, white-trash dinner rolls/hamburger buns.

9 When the pav bhaji has finished simmering and it's tasting all nice and delicious-like, throw it in a bowl and top it with those quick-marinated onions. Use bread as your utensil and go to work.

LOADED AVOCADO FRIES

SERVES 4

1 quart vegetable oil, for frying

4 slightly underripe avocados

3½ cups flour

1 egg

1½ cups ice-cold beer

1 shot vodka (plus more for personal drinking)

1 Roma tomato, diced

½ red onion, diced

1 jalapeño, diced

1 tablespoon minced cilantro

1 can refried beans

¼ cup crumbled queso fresco (leave out if you want to get vegan with it)

Jalapeño rings and hot sauce, for serving

I've done a few short-term vegan stints in my life. The first was to explicitly try and lose weight after my track career was finished: I lost 25 pounds in four weeks surviving on almonds and cigarettes. A few months later I decided I wanted to try and abstain from animal products for a little while longer, just to see how my body reacted to the shift. Vegans are always talking about how great they feel, and I wanted in. They shouldn't get all the good feeling. I wanted some too, dammit.

I tried eating a more sustainable diet filled with foods like vegetables and grains and beans and anything other than tree nuts and tobacco. I had a fucking blast. I made kimchi fried rice tacos one night, and then a mock cheesesteak with charred portobello mushrooms and cashew cheese spread the next day. I didn't even feel limited. If anything, I was eating more freely than ever.

After six weeks, I stepped on the scale. I had gained 15 pounds. In six weeks. Eating completely vegan. And it's all because of stupid bullshit incredibly delicious recipes like this tricking me into thinking they're healthy just because they're ethical. Shine on, veganism, you crazy diamond.

1 In a large Dutch oven, saucepot, or deep fryer, heat up the quart of vegetable oil. You want to shoot for 375°F.

2 Slice the avocados in half with a paring knife and remove the pits. Use a spoon to cleanly scoop out all the avocado meat. (Is it called meat? Yeah, fuck it, it's called meat.) Cut the avocado meats into 5 strips per half. They should look almost like—wait for it—fries. Boom.

3 Set out two large mixing bowls. In the first, throw in 2 cups of the flour. In the second, combine the egg with the remaining 1½ cups flour, 1½ cups beer, and the shot of vodka. Violently whisk it all together.

4 Take your avocado fries and dredge them in the flour, then gently drag the floury avocado fries through the beer batter, making sure to coat every inch of each. Toss about six of the fries into the fryer, one by one, making sure they don't touch each other at entry. When wet batter sticks to wet batter, you get a shitty time. It should only take about 30 seconds for them to get golden brown and crispy—you don't want them to fry too long and get super-hot, brown avocado—at which point you should remove them from the fryer and let drain on a nest of paper towels. Repeat the process until they're all fried.

5 Mix the tomato, onion, jalapeño, and cilantro in a bowl. This is called pico de gallo. If you're a functioning human in society, you should know that. Also, open up that can of refried beans and warm them in a small sauté pan on the stove. If you like them soupy like I do, add 2 tablespoons water.

6 Arrange the avocado fries in a bowl, then top with (soupy) refried beans, pico de gallo, queso fresco, jalapeño rings, and a hot sauce of your choice.

SOYRIZO Y PAPAS
TACOS

——

MAKES 12 TACOS

Vegetable oil, for cooking

3 large russet potatoes, peeled and ½-inch diced

Salt

Black pepper

1 (12-ounce) tube vegetarian chorizo (Soyrizo)

12 corn tortillas

½ cup diced cabbage

½ white onion, minced

2 tablespoons minced cilantro

2 limes, cut into wedges

There is no single greater vegetarian ingredient on the planet than Soyrizo. I'll even use it in place of regular pork chorizo just for shits. It has all the same spices as that earthy, spicy, funky Mexican sausage, and it gives you roughly the same texture and eating experience with about one quarter the calories and 100 percent less lymph nodes and salivary glands.

The first time I made these tacos I was at a bachelor party. Because where else are you going to develop vegetable-centric recipes, am I right? We had 16 guys staying in a massive Airbnb in Austin, Texas, and I was tasked with cooking a giant taco spread for our first day in the city. But there was a catch—we had a vegan on board. Whoaaaaa! Everyone seemed super-worried about what Vegan Mike was going to eat—except for me and Vegan Mike.

I voted to make the entire feast vegan and just Colicchio the shit out of them plant tacos, but people started throwing out words like *al pastor* and *pollo asado* and a carnivorous bloodlust took hold. So Vegan Mike was left with one option: *Soyrizo y papas*, an ethical take on the classic spicy sausage and potato combo. I made a fuckton because I really wanted to eat some too, and they were the first dish to be eighty-sixed. Those selfish omnivore sonsabitches ate them so fast that I didn't get one. Suck it, people who lack imagination and use meat as a crutch. Suck on this Soyrizo dick.

1 Heat a sauté pan on medium-high heat and pour in ½ inch of vegetable oil. When the oil starts to shimmer and looks like it's alive, add the potatoes. Don't worry too much about overcrowding or working in batches. You're not going for perfection here; you just need to get some shit cooked and moderately crispy. Season the potatoes with salt and pepper and keep them moving around the pan for about 15 minutes, until they're nice and golden brown. Drain the oil from the pan so you're just left with potato. Again, don't shoot for perfection. You'll just fall short of it and realize you're largely a disappointment.

2 Put the pan back on medium-high heat and ejaculate your tube of scientifically perfect fake chorizo in there. Break up the faux-rizo as best as you can without mashing the potatoes and continue to sauté for another 5 minutes.

3 **Heat up the tortillas any way you know how:** Throw them in a hot pan, or wrap them in wet paper towels in stacks of six and microwave for 15 seconds. You just do you here. Mix the cabbage, onion, and cilantro in a bowl.

4 Throw down some of your potato and veggie chorizo slop onto a tortilla, top it with some of your cabbage mix, squeeze some lime on it, and you got yourself some crunchy vegan munchies right there.

MUSHROOM TOAST

with
Blue Cheese
Whipped Cream

SERVES 4

12 ounces maitake mushrooms
  (if you can't find maitakes, use
  portobellos or creminis)

2 tablespoons vegetable oil

¼ cup minced shallots

2 tablespoons chopped fresh
  thyme

½ stick (4 tablespoons) butter

Salt

Cracked black pepper

1 lemon, sliced in half through the
  equator

12 ounces heavy whipping cream,
  very cold

6 ounces blue cheese

1 loaf super-hipster artisanal
  bread

There are several reasons to start cooking, and no one reason is more important than another. Your motivation can stem from necessity, or a genuine interest in food, or the need to impress people, or you can be drunk or stoned and just want some dopetastic lunchie munchies. All are incredibly valid reasons to get in the kitchen.

Personally, I've found there's one driving force more powerful than the rest: crippling stress and anxiety that makes you feel like your entire world is going to crumble unless you can solve a puzzle and claim a sense of power and ownership over a basic task. Food has always been that task for me. I call it procrasti-cooking.

Whenever I procrasti-cook, the weird shit starts to come out of the woodwork. Combinations I never would have thought to try—but if I try them and they work, then that's the equivalent of hitting a fucking stress-relieving homerun ball. A puzzle solved.

This blue cheese whipped cream went straight into the upper deck. It's such a simple thing, but it tastes like nothing you've ever had before: creamy and airy and funky, and when it starts to melt down the sides of that toast, there's nothing like it.

---

1 Wipe the mushrooms down with a damp paper towel and then start butchering them. If you're using maitakes, the bunch of mushrooms is really only connected by the large stem at the bottom. You want to try and keep as much of it intact as possible, so cut each piece to have part of the stem attached. You're inevitably going to get some mushroom bits flaking off, but keeping them relatively intact is still the goal. You want the main pieces of 'shroom to be about 1½ inches long.

2 When your mushrooms are butchered, heat the vegetable oil in a large, heavy-bottomed saucepan on high heat. When the oil starts to smoke—you want this shit hot—drop in some of the mushrooms, making sure not to overcrowd the pan. Sear for about 1 minute on each side, until deeply browned. Maybe even get some black on it. Take the seared mushrooms out of the pan and start on the next batch.

3 When the last round of mushrooms is finished searing, quickly throw the shallots, thyme, and butter into the pan, and add back all your mushrooms. Season up with salt and black pepper, and continue to sauté on high heat for another 2 minutes, until the shallots are translucent. Turn the heat off, add the juice of half the lemon, and give it a good toss to coat.

4 Throw the cream—make sure it's ice cold—blue cheese, 1 teaspoon salt, and ½ teaspoon black pepper into the food processor. Let it run on high for about a minute, until it sticks to the bowl.

5 Slice bread. Then toast it.

6 Top the toast with mushrooms and dollops of blue cheese whipped cream and serve with the remaining half lemon on the side for ad hoc squeezing. The whipped cream is going to start melting when it hits the hot mushrooms and it's fucking wild. You'll love it.

**MUSHROOM TOAST WITH
BLUE CHEESE WHIPPED
CREAM,** *page 59*

ORANGE
CAULIFLOWER
NUGGETS

SERVES 4

1 quart vegetable oil, for frying;
 plus 1 tablespoon

3 cups cornstarch

2 eggs

1 cup beer

2 teaspoons salt

1 head cauliflower, cut into florets

3 Thai chilies, minced; plus
 additional sliced chilies for
 garnish

1 tablespoon minced shallot

2 cloves garlic, minced

1 tablespoon grated ginger

3 big-ass oranges

¼ cup soy sauce

¼ cup rice wine vinegar

¼ cup sugar

½ teaspoon sesame oil

White rice, for serving

Roasted sesame seeds and thinly
 sliced scallions, for garnish

If you go to a steam-table Chinese restaurant and get anything other than the candy-fried chicken—orange chicken, General Tso's chicken, lemon chicken, sesame chicken, it's all the same—you're doing it wrong. Well, that's not true—you're allowed a honey walnut shrimp, or beef and broccoli, or kung pao chicken once every three visits but only to remind you how good candy-fried chicken is. That said, if you were to really boil down the essence of what's so great about candy meat, it has everything to do with the candy, and almost nothing to do with the meat, yeah? Think about it: There could be literally anything inside that crispy coating and you wouldn't even notice it after that sweet, spicy, acidic orange coating tongue-punches you in the flavor button. Might as well spare a chicken's life and senselessly murder a cauliflower head instead.

1 Heat that quart of vegetable oil on medium-high heat in whatever-the-fuck-vessel you use to fry foods. You want the oil to be 350°F.

2 Get out two mixing bowls. Fill the first with cornstarch, and fill the second with the eggs and beer and whisk them together. Put a teaspoon of salt in each and mix, just in case.

3 Take the cauliflower florets and dredge them in the cornstarch, then give them a quick bath in the wet ingredients, then get them back into the cornstarch, and really work to press the cornstarch into every nook and cranny. You want complete coverage here.

4 Drop the cauliflower nuggets into the fryer, making sure you don't overcrowd the pan. That would be bad. Fry for about 6 minutes each batch, until they're a deep golden brown. Don't let the oil get above 350°F, because you need to fry these for a long enough time that the cauliflower steams itself from the inside out. Raw cauliflower tastes like farts, and you don't want to eat farts.

5 Let the cauliflower nuggets drain on a paper towel and then start building your sauce. Heat that tablespoon of vegetable oil on high heat in a large sauté pan and when it starts to shimmer, add the chilies, shallot, garlic, and ginger. Stir with a wooden spoon so it doesn't burn and everything gets evenly sweated, about 5 minutes.

6 While that's happening, juice all three oranges into some sort of bowl or something, and then pour that into the pan, along with the soy sauce, vinegar, sugar, sesame oil, and 1 cup water. Whisk it all together in the pan, let come to a boil, and reduce for 5 or 6 minutes, until the sauce sticks to the back of a spoon. If you want the sauce to be a little bit tighter, sprinkle ½ teaspoon leftover cornstarch into the sauce and stir quickly to avoid lumps.

7 When the sauce is done reducing, keep it on the heat, throw in your cauliflower nuggets, and give them a good toss in the sauce. Serve on top of white rice (or not, I have no dog in this fight) and garnish with some sesame seeds, scallions, and some slices of Thai chili if you're really trying to get froggy.

BROCCOLINI
with
Burnt Lemon
Hollandaise

SERVES 4

1 pound broccolini, aka baby broccoli

¼ cup vegetable oil

Salt

Coarse ground black pepper

1 lemon, sliced in half through the equator

1 stick (8 tablespoons) plus 1 tablespoon butter

½ cup panko breadcrumbs

2 tablespoons minced chives

2 egg yolks

This recipe is a master class in how to immediately modernize your food and raise its value while effectively doing nothing to inconvenience you. First: Never use regular broccoli again. What's the point? It's worse than broccolini in every single way. It tastes less good, it looks less cool, and it makes you seem less intelligent. (Broccoli is way cheaper though, so don't let me shame you into altering your grocery budget.) Second: Burn your citrus. I have a general disdain (but also secret reverence) for cheap kitchen tricks that make your food seem more interesting, but charring off lemons is the real deal. The natural sugars start to caramelize, you get that little bit of oxidized funk, and the heat tempers the acid a bit so you can get more lemon flavor without any unwanted sourness. It just makes your shit taste better. Trust me.

There is one, super-inconvenient, super-worth-it step here though: You need to make a hollandaise from scratch. I know, I know, it blows, but you have to do it. There's just no substitute. That 15-second eggless blender hollandaise recipe that you found on Pinterest is trash and so is the triple peppermint fudge pretzel mug cake recipe on the board next to it. This is good life practice though—it builds character.

---

1 Burn some broccolini! Heat your oven to 450°F. Trim the broccolini stems, but don't completely get rid of them. Just trim the shitty, woody part of the end.

2 Put the broccolini in a large mixing bowl, then toss in the vegetable oil, 1 teaspoon salt, and 1 teaspoon pepper. Massage all the salt and pepper and oil deep into the broccolini crowns. Place on a baking sheet and throw it in the oven. After 10 minutes, flip all the broccolini, then continue to cook for another 5 or 6 minutes on the other side. You want some good burn. Burn is good. When it's done, turn the oven off, crack the door, and let the broccolini stay warm in there.

3 Burn a lemon! Burn all the things! Heat a cast-iron pan on super-hot for like 5 minutes, and when it's all nice and dangerous, put the lemons cut-side down in the pan and sear for 4 minutes. When you pull them off, the flesh should be nice and pleasantly burnt.

4 Melt 1 tablespoon of the butter in a small sauté pan over medium heat, then add the panko. Sauté for 2 to 3 minutes, until the panko has slightly darkened in color. Add ½ teaspoon salt and a few cracks of black pepper, turn off the heat, and toss in the chives.

5 You need to set up a double boiler. Fill a large stockpot with 2 inches of water, heat it on high, bring it to a boil, then drop the heat to low. Sounds arbitrary, but do it.

6 Put the yolks in a metal mixing bowl that's large enough to rest comfortably on the mouth of the boiling stockpot. Discard the whites, or drink them for some much-needed gainz.

7 Juice half of the burnt lemon into the bowl with the egg yolks and whisk the fuck out of it. I mean all fucks, completely gone. You're actually looking to beat air into the yolks, which is going to make it easier to emulsify the butter into them. The mixture should almost double in size. Also, you should meanwhile put that whole stick of butter in a small pot and heat over low heat until melted, then turn off the heat and reserve.

8 Fuck. Finally. Make some hollandaise: Place the mixing bowl with the yolks on top of the simmering stockpot, then slowly stream in the melted butter while whisking constantly. If the yolk starts to curdle, take the bowl off the heat for a second and turn the burner down. If the butter isn't properly mixing with the yolk, turn the heat up a little and whisk more violently. It's an intricate dance.

9 When all your butter is incorporated and emulsified, turn off the heat. Your hollandaise should have the texture of a loose custard. If it's too thick and fudgy, just add a few drops of water and whisk. It probably needs salt too. Add some salt until it tastes good.

10 Spread the broccolini out on a serving platter, spoon your hollandaise over the top, and top the whole thing with your toasted panko. Serve it with the other half of that burnt lemon and watch everyone swoon. Because they will.

BRAISED BEET BARBACOA

SERVES 4

2 dried ancho chilies

4 dried California chilies

2 large red beets

1 tablespoon vegetable oil

4 scallions, minced

2 tablespoons white vinegar

2 tablespoons fish sauce (this is not vegetarian, but it is delicious)

1 teaspoon Worcestershire (this is also not vegetarian, but it is also delicious)

4 cloves garlic, minced

1 tablespoon cocoa powder

1 teaspoon black pepper

1 teaspoon ground cumin

Salt

Tortillas, rice and beans, bread, etc., for serving

Cilantro, for garnish

I don't want to get all preachy about this; just know in advance that I'm better than you and you're a monster who's single-handedly responsible for the destruction of the American family farm as an institution and, by association, the environment. Unless you're also part of a community-supported agriculture program. If you are, carry on then. And good on you.

I pay money to get a big-ass box of vegetables from local farms delivered to my house. It makes me feel good inside, even though I've done zero research on what farms the food is actually coming from. But what I love even more than the self-righteousness—and I do love the self-righteousness—is that I get a *chopped* basket on my doorstep every week.

This week's basket had red beets, some monster scallions, and garlic, and then I had a fuckton of dried chilies to use up. And it turned out to be one of my very favorite (almost) vegetarian recipes. Does it have anything to do with actual barbacoa, the Mexican dish typically made with a whole cow's head? Nope. But if Chipotle can use the word to refer to a bunch of shredded stuff in spicy sauce, so can I.

1 Heat a large sauté pan on medium-high heat. Stem and seed the dried chilies, then give them a rough chop until they're in 2-inch pieces. Throw down the chilies in the hot pan and toast until they've become slightly darker in color and smell fragrant and dopetasic but not burnt, about 5 minutes.

2 Bring 3 cups water to a boil in a saucepot, then throw in the toasted chilies. After 3 minutes, turn the heat off, stir the chilies, pop a lid on there, and let sit for at least 15 minutes.

3 Meanwhile, peel the beets. If you have a mandoline, use it to slice the beets into the thinnest possible sheets. If not, do your best with a knife. I know I don't say this often enough, but...I believe in you, son. Take those thin beet sheets, stack them up, and slice them to create very thin beet strips.

4 When your chilies have softened, throw them, along with the water they've been sitting in, into the food processor. Let it run on high for at least 2 minutes.

5 Place the vegetable oil in a large Dutch oven or any other heavy-bottomed pot you have. You can even use a sauté pan as long as it's big enough. Place on high heat, and when the oil shimmers and shakes, throw down your beets and scallions and sauté for 2 minutes.

6 Toss in the vinegar, fish sauce, Worcestershire, garlic, cocoa powder, black pepper, and cumin and sauté until some of the mixture has caramelized on the bottom of the pan, about 2 minutes. Throw in all that chili puree, give it a good stir, and cook on medium heat until almost all the liquid has evaporated from the pan, about 30 minutes.

7 Add salt to taste, then serve on a bed of rice and black beans and garnish with cilantro leaves. Or put it in a tortilla. Or make a sandwich out of it. Ball's in your court now, bro.

WAKE &
Bake

THE
RITUAL
of
Brunch

▶ I don't personally believe in breakfast. I mean, I believe it exists, I just don't believe in practicing it. On a typical weekday, I'll wake up to 32 ounces of coffee, eat a garbage protein bar at around 3 p.m. when my stomach starts rumbling so loud that it distracts me from the trap music blasting in my headphones (sometimes I think it's just bass though), then I'll go home and binge-eat whatever the fuck I want.

When athletes do this, it's called intermittent fasting. When I do this, it's called disordered eating. Whatever—potato, potato (you have to pronounce those two differently to get the effect). It's the most emotionally satisfying way to eat. You should try it sometime.

The weekends are a different story. It's a free-for-all—a brunch-tastic battle royale of throwing eggs and hollandaise and maple syrup on whatever mounds of food I can get my hands on. I'll still do the one-meal-a-day thing, but it generally involves consuming 3,000 or more calories of butter, liquor, and cured pork products at 11:30 a.m. and then melting into a drunken food coma for the next 12 to 22 hours.

Our ritual of brunch was perfected in Santa Barbara. Whenever the first of us woke up on a weekend morning, still probably drunk from the night before, we'd run through both floors of the duplex to see if we could find at least one person out of the ten available to make a Costco run to forage for brunch supplies. All menu planning was done in the car on the way over.

I would come home, bang on the door as violently as possible so I could wake at least three people up, and put them on prep duty. That might have been marinating meat for the carne asada home fries, or setting up an egg-poaching station for waffle Benedicts, or shredding sweet potatoes for some sugary dessert latkes.

Dave and Abe would always make a *tortilla española*—a big-ass Spanish potato, egg, and onion frittata—because I think one of them went to Spain at some point and they could bang it out perfectly every time.

Rickards always took on the very important task of mixing up a five-gallon Gatorade cooler full of bromosas. You might not know what a bromosa is, because it doesn't really exist, and also it has no business existing. The recipe is simple: Pour equal parts cheap orange juice, cheaper champagne, and cheapest vodka in a vat, except make sure there's more vodka than any of the other parts, and then pour some more vodka in.

Our Last Supper–style brunch table belonged to a law firm that decided they wanted to give away an absolute dime-piece of furniture for zero dollars on Craigslist. We put it on the roof of my Ford Taurus and held it down with our hands for all the ten miles of bumpy side-street driving on the way back.

That table became our nexus, and it never saw more use than during a brunch orgy. The entire 12-foot-long surface would be

tastes like—sweet, fragrant, heady—until you taste it being exuded from ham fat every time you close your mouth to chew. We all gagged trying to get down our first piece. The ham was almost edible after we lit it on fire with a blowtorch. You live and you learn.

We would generally drink and shoot the shit and try to retrace our steps from the night before to figure out why our house was so fucked up that particular morning. An Irish rugby player once punched a hole in our wall during a party, but none of us could remember how the hole got there until we put our heads together over some bromosas and eggs. That guy was cool, too. Still don't know why he did it.

It was more than encouraged to excuse yourself from the brunch table to take a nap underneath it, or to go body-surfing to burn off some of the pork fat, then come back and hit the spread hard again. Friends would roll through, strangers would roll through, alumni trying to relive their glory days would roll through, and we would just spend the entire day holding court at that table.

Breakfast is profane; brunch is sacred.

covered in bagels, smoked salmon, cream cheese, bacon, sausages, waffles, eggs, hash browns, French toast, jugs of syrup, gas station sushi, beers, and bromosa cups.

The food wasn't always great, but batting a thousand isn't exactly realistic. The rum ham debacle of 2012 is still a low point in all of our lives. Or maybe it's a high point, looking back. It's hard to tell. We thought it would be a great idea to soak an entire spiral ham in rum, because that way we could take it to the beach— literally 50 yards from our front lawn—and get shit-housed off cured pork and no one would know.

It was inspired by an episode of *It's Always Sunny in Philadelphia*. The character who makes rum ham also eats cat food and once tried to put out a grease fire with a handgun. He is a very good role model, so this seemed like a good idea. You think you know what rum

FIVE-STEP
Hocnover
Cure

There is no scientific way to cure a hangover. It doesn't exist. Spicy food, greasy food, charcoal tablets, hair of the dog—all of that is complete bullshit, though I'll honor the pseudoscientific reasoning from the hair-of-the-dog crowd because I respect anyone trying to slam shots of bourbon at 9 a.m. on a Sunday. Do whatever you need to do to get through the day, man.

The only way to make the sun not feel like a baseball bat being smashed over your face after a drinking binge is to wait it out, chug a bunch of water (which isn't even specific to hangovers, you should just be doing that anyways), and take ibuprofen to tranquilize the cymbal-playing clockwork monkey trapped inside your head.

"So, Josh, Mr. Fucking Drinking Expert, that's your advice? Just sit there and do nothing?"

No, no, no no no. Absolutely not. If I listened to things like "science" or "facts" or "doctors," I probably wouldn't do/consume half the things that I do currently do/consume. You think low-carb diets and workout supplements are backed by modern medicine? Not even a little bit.

My strategy to beat a hangover is to ensure quality of life rather than go on a wild-goose chase trying to treat the symptoms. The real key to getting yourself back to normal is self-care: making yourself as happy as possible in whatever form that may take. Here are the things that I've learned work for me, and they just might work for you too.

1
ENERGY DRINK

You have to get one of the real dirty ones too. I'm not talking about a 5-Hour Energy shot or a Red Bull—I mean one of those 240-plus-mg-of-caffeine bootleg-looking tallboy cans. If it has an endorsement sticker from the UFC, that's a bonus point. Since caffeine gets you all riled up, one of these cans of liquid lightning should put you back to normal operating speed.

2
GREASY SANDWICH

This has nothing to do with pretending that fatty or calorie-rich foods can help cure your hangover on the biological level. Greasy sandwiches just happen to be my favorite thing in the world to eat, and when I'm feeling like shit—physically, emotionally, or otherwise—I need a basic mood elevator. It's like how Harry Potter eats a chocolate frog after a dementor tries to tongue-kiss his soul out of his body or whatever, except my chocolate frog is a double cheeseburger stuffed with bacon, jalapeño poppers, and a fried egg. And my dementor is my own poor decision making. Shit, that got deep real fast.

3
SHITTY REGGAE

I'm not saying that reggae is shitty, I'm saying that you need to listen to a particularly shitty brand of reggae. Park your ass in the comfiest chair in the darkest room that you can find and softly play some Rebelution or Slightly Stoopid. People apparently like their music, but it isn't good. And that's what you need right now—something neutral and vaguely calming to act as background noise. Anything that you enjoy too much is going to raise the humors and get you all worked up. It's not time for that yet. This is the calm before the storm. The energy drink made you functional, the sandwich made you happy, and now the shitty reggae is going to make you tranquil.

4
MINDLESS VIDEO GAME

Choose a game that you can play with your eyes closed and crank the difficulty settings all the way to the left. You want it to be as easy as possible. The goal here is to slowly and gently build your confidence back up by solving childishly easy problems with no effort. Personally, I play FIFA against the computer on amateur mode and just let Cristiano Ronaldo fucking run wild on the pitch.

5
INTENSELY EMOTIONAL MOVIE

You are in a good state right now, but you can't be fat and euphoric your whole life. You need to snap out of it. You need an emotional purge. Don't cop out and put on some sappy bullshit like *Marley & Me*. Really dig deep for something heavy—a movie that makes you realize the world is a nightmare and you have to do something about it. Something like *Dear Zachary: A Letter to a Son About His Father,* or *Once Were Warriors,* or the film that kicked off this tradition: *For Colored Girls.* When Beau Willie (spoiler alert:) drops the kids out the apartment window to their deaths, I literally jumped out of my chair, screamed "NOOOOOOOOO," and collapsed on the floor crying. Then half an hour later I was ready to take on the day. Boom. Hangover cured.

A VERY AMERICAN BREAKFAST SHAKE

SERVES 2

1 pint vanilla ice cream

3 frosted strawberry toaster pastries

4 scoops whey protein powder

2 tablespoons almond butter

½ cup fruit cereal

2 cups whole milk

4 large ice cubes

This should only be consumed immediately following a high-volume workout when your glycogen stores have been completely depleted and you need some serious carb power to give you that insulin spike, which, as we all know, increases amino acid transport efficiency into the muscle cell, creating an optimal anabolic environment. Or, if you're really stoney baloney. You can make it then, too.

When I actually gave a shit about being strong and athletic and all that—the long long ago when I threw heavy rocks all day instead of sitting on my ass and writing about chalupas—different variations on this shake were my go-to following Saturday morning lifting sessions. Don't feel beholden to this exact recipe (or any recipe in this book; take control of your own destiny, dammit).

Once you have a base of protein powder, milk, ice, and nut butter, feel free to experiment with any combination of cereals and pastries. One of my favorite variations came from an impromptu McDonald's stop. I threw an apple pie and two whole soft-serve ice creams—cones included—into the blender and it came out fantastic. Ditto for the Butterfinger and Count Chocula version. So grab either a barbell or a bong and start doing some research.

1 Put all that shit in a blender.

2 Blend.

3 Drink.

4 Get swole.

5 ????????

6 Profit.

HASH BROWNS MADAME

SERVES 4

1 package frozen hash brown patties, the McDonald's-shaped kind (You'll need 8 total hash brown patties)

2 tablespoons butter, plus more for frying

1½ tablespoons flour

2 cups whole milk

1 teaspoon salt

½ teaspoon black pepper

4 eggs

8 ounces thin-sliced quality ham

12 ounces shredded Gruyère cheese

Ketchup, for serving

Hash browns are potatoes in their perfect form. And I'm not talking about the diner-style stuff where you see shreds of real potato, and you can kind of reverse engineer it in your mind to imagine what they may have looked like as things growing in the ground. I'm talking about your average, deep-fry-able fast-food hash brown patty that has never existed as a collection of raw ingredients. They just sort of spawn into frozen, golden-brown existence.

Ideologically, they share similarities to Tater Tots, but they differ architecturally, which is key for this dish. Hash brown patties have more surface area than tots, and their unique flat shape makes them perfect for stacking and stuffing. Which is why, as you can see from this recipe, I have decided to use them as sandwich buns for the French bistro classic Croque Madame—a ham and cheese sandwich smothered in béchamel and topped with a fried egg. Except this is better, because fried potatoes. America!

1 Bake the hash brown patties according to the directions on the package. For those of you inquiring about the efficacy of frozen potato products, let me briefly say—go fuck your own face, you bougie impractical piece of shit.

2 Cool. So yeah, that's why. Making your own hash browns is hard and they never come out that good, despite how you keep telling yourself that next time they're going to turn out differently. No they won't. People don't change.

3 While the hash browns are cooking, make yourself a béchamel. In a small saucepot, heat the 2 tablespoons butter over medium heat. When it's melted, add the flour and stir together for about 2 minutes, until the flour is completely incorporated and it starts to smell a little roasty. Add in the milk, salt, and pepper, then whisk together and continue to simmer for an additional 2 minutes, or until the sauce can coat the back of a spoon.

4 Fry up the eggs over-easy in some more butter. I don't have any good tips for you. You should probably just watch a YouTube tutorial, honestly.

5 Throw your broiler on high. Place a bed of hash brown patties on the bottom of any heat-proof pan, blanket them in ham slices, then Gruyère and a bit of béchamel. Just a wee bit. Top with another layer of hash browns, then slather those in béchamel. Broil for about 4 minutes, or until that delicious white goo starts to burn.

6 Top the Francophilic slop bucket with some fried eggs. You should probably put some ketchup on it, too.

DONUT HOLES

with
Maple–Bacon Fat Buttercream

MAKES 12 DONUT HOLES

1 pound store-bought pizza dough (making things from scratch is hard)

12 ounces bacon

1 quart vegetable oil, for frying

2 cups powdered sugar, plus ¼ cup for dusting

2 tablespoons quality fake maple syrup (I use Aunt Jemima Lite)

1 tablespoon whipping cream

Look, if you're really feeling ambitious, and if dropping a bunch of pizza dough in the fryer early in the morning makes you uncomfortable, then, by all means, make some donut dough from scratch. I won't begrudge you your right to do that.

But I will not stand around and watch as you shit all over the good name of Giada De Laurentiis. I got this half-assed shortcut idea from an OG episode of *Giada at Home* where she makes fake *zeppoli* (apparently that means "donut" in Italian) by frying store-bought pizza dough and rolling it in sugar, but it's cool because it was for her kid's preschool class's finger-painting party or whatever and kids are stupid and all they want to eat are boogers and mac and cheese so how would they ever know the difference.

I am also stupid. Stupid like a fox. Are these the best donuts you've ever had? Nope. Yeah, no, not even a little bit. That's why you have to bury your shame under a mountain of super-dope buttercream that's laced with an obscene amount of bacon fat. Oh, but if anyone asks, just tell them you made the dough from scratch. Lying is generally a good policy.

---

1 Make sure your pizza dough is at room temperature. Form it into about 12 balls that are about 1 inch in diameter. Cover with plastic wrap and let them hang out while you do the other shit.

2 Slice the bacon into 1-inch pieces and throw it in a large sauté pan. Cook on medium heat, but make sure to not let the pan get too hot and scorch your meats. Sauté the bacon until all the fat has rendered. Place a colander on top of a large mixing bowl and pour the contents of the pan in there. The goal is to strain all your bacon grease. You can save the bacon meat nuggets for another recipe, or just eat them right there on the spot, which is what you're going to do anyways.

3 You should have about a cup of bacon grease. That's a good amount to make the buttercream. Throw the bowl in the freezer for 15 to 20 minutes, until it comes to slightly above room temperature.

4 While the fat is cooling, heat the vegetable oil (for the donut frying) in a large, heavy-bottomed pot until it reaches 350°F. Or use a deep fryer. That should be obvious by now, yeah?

5 Mix the powdered sugar, maple syrup, and cream into the bowl of bacon fat and whisk the shit out of it for 3 minutes. I mean you really have to go hard here. Switch hands halfway through so you can get even forearm swoleness going on. Or just use one of those electric hand beaters for the same amount of time if you don't feel like getting jacked. The buttercream should have the consistency of a slightly runny frosting, but it will stiffen up as the bacon fat turns back to solid. Use a spoonula to scoop it into a gallon-size Ziploc bag. (Or don't. See step 8 below.) Cut the corner off the bag so you have an opening to squirt the contents out of.

6 Drop about 4 or 5 dough balls in the 350-degree oil. Fry for about 3 minutes, trying your best to rotate the balls continuously, until golden brown. Pull the donuts out and let them rest on some paper towels to drain. Repeat to fry all the balls.

7 When the donut holes have cooled enough to work with, take a paring knife or steak knife and stab a hole through the side into the middle of one, then twist and jimmy it around to create an opening. That's where your meat sugar is going to go. Stab the piping bag tip deep into the donut, and squeeze out the bacon fat buttercream until the donut is filled. Repeat with all the donut holes.

8 If you're not using a Ziploc piping bag, just slice a big opening into the donut and use a small spoon to jam the buttercream in there. Or don't even bother filling them, and just swipe the dough into your fat and sugar goo after every bite. I can't tell you what to do with your life.

9 Dust the donuts with powdered sugar, eat a half dozen, and you're well on your way to a healthy day there, friend.

**DONUT HOLES WITH
MAPLE–BACON FAT
BUTTERCREAM,** *page 78*

Making a proper bacon weave is an absolutely essential skill. Some French chefs make sure their cooks can turn a proper omelet or cut chives with exacting precision—if I were running a restaurant kitchen, I would make sure all my underlings could make a tight-butthole bacon weave with absolutely no residual space in between cross hatches. God, I would be a terrible chef. I'd be mean, too. Go real Gordon Ramsay on my cooks if they fucked up. "Oy, tosser, what the fuck is this then, yeah? Got your fucking sobbles in a bandy haven't you? Jesus. Wake up, you toffee-nosed fucking wank." That's how British people talk in my head. If you just follow the instructions in the recipe, and maybe look up a YouTube bacon-weave tutorial or three, you should have no problem making these carb-light, trans-fat-heavy tortilla proxies.

BACON-WEAVE
TATER TOT
TACOS

SERVES 4

36 ounces bacon (three standard packages)

1 (32-ounce) bag frozen Tater Tots

1 cup shredded cheddar cheese

½ cup sour cream

¼ cup chopped chives

Hot sauce, for finishing

1 Ooooh, you get to make a bacon weave. This is exciting. I hope you're as excited as I am. You should be. Preheat your oven to 350°F. Lay out six strips of bacon on a large baking sheet running parallel to each other and touching at the sides. Then take one strip of bacon and start to thread it through the bottom edge of your bacon square. It will go on top of the first strip of bacon, then under the second, then over the third, then under the fourth—you get it. Take your next slice of bacon, and weave it through right next to the first woven strip, but the opposite—*under* the first, *over* the second, etc. Complete this process until you have a perfect cross-hatched bacon weave. Repeat the process and make two more.

2 Bake the weaves at 350°F for 15 minutes on one side, then flip and bake for an additional 10. You don't want them to get too crispy because these are going to act as your taco shell. They need to fold.

3 Go ahead and cook up those tots. I would recommend deep-frying them, or, if you're tryna bake, throw them in a single layer onto a baking sheet greased up with vegetable oil, drizzle some more oil on top of the tots, and bake at 425°F for 25 minutes. Just, for fuck's sake, please don't microwave them. Actually, whatever, go ahead and do it.

4 When your bacon weaves are cool enough to work with, throw them on a cutting board, and use either a large ring mold or the edge of a wide-mouthed cup to cut them into perfect 4-inch circles. Eat the excess bacon.

5 You should now have about 12 perfect bacon-weave taco shells. Fill each with a few Tater Tots, some cheddar cheese, a dollop of sour cream, and a sprinkling of chives. Because vegetables.

6 Hot sauce.

GRAPEFRUIT & MEZCAL-CURED LOX

MAKES ENOUGH LOX
FOR 4 BAGELS

1 (2-pound) Atlantic salmon fillet, skin on (you'll likely have some salmon left over)

½ cup salt

¼ cup grated grapefruit zest (about 2 large grapefruits' worth)

2 tablespoons sugar

¼ cup chopped fresh dill

¼ cup mezcal (or tequila if you can't find it)

Bagels, cream cheese, and thinly sliced red onion, for serving

Normally I think cooking with hard liquor sucks dicks. Whiskey BBQ sauce, tequila lime chicken, bourbon blueberry what-the-fuck-ever—it's all gimmicky bullshit that never actually makes the food taste better. Why not just eat some ribs and drink a glass of dark liquor? Why do they need to be combined?

It's like edibles: I'd so much rather smoke weed and munch on brownies than eat brownies that taste like burnt fart and will get you so fucked up that you have to run out of a movie theater halfway through Disney Pixar's *Brave* to throw up in a urinal (ask me about that story sometime).

However! This recipe is an exception to the rule, because it actually, y'know, makes sense. I love any sort of raw-textured fish slapped on a bagel—my Bubby Lily is very proud of me embracing my heritage—but smoked salmon always tastes like acrid knockoff bacon, and straight-up salt-cured salmon has no depth.

That's where mezcal comes into play. It's naturally super smoky, and the medicinal notes play off the bitterness of grapefruit, which is all rounded out by fatty salmon and fresh dill. Also, since alcohol kills bacteria, I think this means you can get away with buying sketchier fish. If it makes you feel better, feel free to buy sushi-grade fish from your local grocery store or fishmonger, but also know that the term sushi-grade is completely unregulated, and largely means nothing.

1 Dry off that salmon fillet real well with some paper towels. In a large mixing bowl, combine the salt, zest, sugar, dill, and mezcal.

2 Lay out a whole bunch of plastic wrap on your cutting board, going three slightly overlapping layers wide and at least a yard long. Put the salmon skin-side down, then pack your salty, fruity, sugary liquor mixture on top, spreading it evenly over the flesh.

3 Wrap the fillet up tightly in the plastic wrap, then throw it in a large casserole dish. You need to put something heavy on top so the flavor stuff really presses into the flesh and the salt can draw out the moisture and cure the fish. I'd recommend using an old college textbook to feel like you finally got your fucking money's worth. Throw the casserole dish in the fridge.

4 After 12 hours, unwrap the fish and drain the liquid. Wrap it back up and let it cure for another 12 hours in the fridge.

5 Thinly slice the salmon against the grain of fat. Spread cream cheese on toasted bagels, then throw on some salmon slices and red onion.

NO-CARB SAUSAGE WAFFLE SANDWICHES

SERVES 4

24 ounces pork breakfast sausage

Nonstick cooking spray

3 tablespoons ketchup

1 tablespoon Sriracha

8 eggs

1 teaspoon salt

½ teaspoon black pepper

2 tablespoons butter

4 slices American cheese

Growing up in the bowels of southern Orange County during peak South Beach Diet hysteria (like if Atkins was designed by the Real Housewives), I was constantly inundated with low-carb propaganda. After a basketball game when I was eight or nine years old, one of the team moms crammed the entire squad into her bright yellow H2 and somehow scraped her way through the In-N-Out drive-through. She ordered something I'd never seen before. It was a burger, because she was eating it with her hands, but it was a salad because it was all lettuce. She told me this was called "protein-style," and that "the bun is the only unhealthy part of In-N-Out, you know." Needless to say, this was a fucking revelation. I could eat anything I wanted—anything at all!—so long as there was no bread in and around my mouth. That one sentence blurted by a Hummer-driving Orange County basketball mom, mouth full of contradictorily carb-heavy ketchup, almost two decades ago has dictated every single food choice I've made since. tl;dr: You can eat as many of these sausage sandwiches as you want and you won't get fat.

1 Lay down a fuckton of paper towels. It's about to get weird. Put your waffle maker on top and crank it all the way up. Divide your breakfast sausage into 8 equal mounds, then form them into patties. Spray some nonstick cooking spray on the waffle maker, then throw down a sausage patty, and forcibly close the waffle maker on it and continue to press down for about 4 minutes, until the sausage is cooked through and sufficiently waffled. There's going to be a good amount of fat seeping out, but that's what the paper towels are for. Repeat the process until all the sausages are waffled.

2 Mix together the ketchup and Sriracha in a little bowl and set aside.

3 In a large mixing bowl, whisk together the eggs, salt, and pepper. Heat the butter in a large nonstick skillet on medium-high heat, then drop in the eggs. Stir constantly with a spatula until the curds start to form, then turn off the heat.

4 Lay down a slice of cheese on top of one of the sausage waffles, then throw roughly a quarter of your eggs on top, which should be enough to melt the cheese. Spoon a little bit of Sriracha ketchup on top of that, add another sausage waffle, and you got yourself a handheld breakfast on-the-go, insofar as you don't mind getting grease on literally everything you touch.

**NO-CARB
SAUSAGE
WAFFLE
SANDWICHES,**
page 85

FRUIT & BROGURT PARFAITS

SERVES 2

2 cups nonfat Greek yogurt

1 scoop of your favorite, heavily flavored preworkout

1 scoop of your favorite, heavily flavored protein powder

2 tablespoons water; or more, depending on thickness

2 bananas, sliced into coins

1 cup blackberries

12 strawberries, hulled and sliced in half

½ cup chopped almonds

¼ cup unsweetened coconut flakes

What is breakfast really all about? Eggs? Pancakes? Coffee? Little pastries with cool swirly patterns and stuff? Wrong. All of that is wrong. Get them the fuck out of here, I don't want to see them again. Breakfast is about efficiency. It's about starting your day with the proper combination of nutrients that is going to fuel you towards being a productive member of society. And by nutrients I mean a bunch of protein and caffeine and beta-alanine and other stuff that's going to get you all riled up and pre-pared for the crushing wall of shit that life is about to topple onto you.

I've done much intense scientific research on what supplements go well with what dairy and grain products. I have found that a combo of yo-gurt and sweetened protein powder (brogurt) is a very good combination. Oatmeal with protein powder (broatmeal) is also very good, but you have to stir the powder in *after* microwaving and not before, or else it turns into chewy, taffy-esque goo.

I have found that cooking creatine into a risotto (brosotto) is a very bad idea, and I think creatine might turn poisonous at certain tempera-tures because it sure tasted like poison. In my science-ing, I also found out that your throat will automatically swell and close itself off to prevent you from swallowing couscous that's been cooked in grape-flavored pre-workout (sorry, no bro wordplay there).

1 In a large bowl, stir together the yogurt, preworkout (I call it "go dust"), and protein powder. The protein powder will thicken the yogurt a bunch, so thin it out with some water until it's back to the original yogurt consistency.

2 In two fancy-as-fuck-looking glass cups—you gotta see the layers, bro!—lay down a base of brogurt, top it with some fruit, then more brogurt, then more fruit, then chopped almonds and coconut flakes.

3 Eat all of it and then go be the best you you can be, or at least like one of the better yous you could be. Like, go out there and be a top-five you. Fuck you, just eat the supplement yogurt.

5

STUFF
Chicks
Like

EVERYTHING
I Know
About
CHICKS

▶ Crafting an overwhelmingly masculine image has been a long and hard (boom, dick stuff!) process that I wasn't always aware of. When I was a kid, I started drinking black coffee because in the back of my mind I knew that men weren't supposed to allow themselves the comfort and pleasure of cream and sugar. I've been drinking my coffee like that ever since. I don't even think about it now, it's just a reflex.

Even though I never had to give it any real thought, gender is still an important part of my identity. It's shaped my worldview, it's added context to my personal relationships, and, like all identities, it's a useful crutch that I can fall back on when I feel vulnerable in any way. I wouldn't trade my status as a dude-bro-guy for the world. I mean, I'd trade it for like $30 and a taco 12-pack, but the point stands: Bro-hood means a lot to me, though only if it's on my own terms.

That's why it bothers me when people try and define masculinity by its antithesis—by the non-feminine. My gender broformance doesn't fully define me as a person; it's not who I am all the time; I don't wear a backwards snapback in my sleep (unless I'm really drunk), and it doesn't negate my (what society would call) feminine qualities or make them any less meaningful. I write a blog about food and my feelings—I'm not exactly trying to be Clint Eastwood here.

Naming the blog *Culinary Bro-Down* was always meant to be a sort of contradiction, or at least a perceived contradiction. I like to drink beer and play pickup football just as much as I like to make white Zinfandel sangria and host *Top Chef* viewing parties (sangria's refreshing as shit; it's like the alcohol gods pissed fruit punch into a carafe full of fresh-cut citrus fruit). And none of those interests should be mutually exclusive. One doesn't have to threaten another.

My love of beer doesn't cancel out my love of wine. My tendency to eat giant cuts of meat doesn't make me any less likely to binge on braised kale. My craving for Taco Bell doesn't negate my want for a full and healthy life. I guess that last one's a little harder to reconcile, what with science and all, but you see my point—things need to be defined by what they are, not by what they aren't.

A personal hero of mine, former NFL quarterback and current activist Don McPherson, said something that really resonated with me: "We don't raise boys to be men. We raise them not to be women." From a young age, we're told to reject any quote-unquote feminine impulses—empathy, vulnerability, emotion in general. We're told how not to exist, not how *to* exist.

Labels can be useful to form your identity and interact with like-minded people, but they shouldn't create boundaries that hold you back from doing things you'd really like to do. Once you let them pigeonhole you, you're totally fucked.

There was a single defining moment in my life where I realized all this gendered policing was complete bullshit. It was my first year at UCLA, as a third-year transfer student, and I was getting ready to go to a party. You know—how college kids do. You've seen movies. It was a track team party, and I told my teammates I'd bring beer because I wanted to seem cool and generous, but mainly cool.

I was still 20 years old, which meant I had to use the janky-ass fake Connecticut driver's license I'd bought off the Internet. When I walked into the grocery store closest to campus, the first thing I saw was a kid getting his fake ID confiscated and begging the cashier—almost in tears—to not call the police. I ran out the door and drove four miles away (30 minutes in L.A. traffic) to a less sketchy store.

I grabbed a 30-pack of Busch Light, because that was our brand of choice in Santa Barbara and I wanted to share a little bit of my personal drinking culture with the people I was going to spend the next three years of my life with. When the cashier quizzed me on my address, I completely blanked. I wasn't able to produce a single word. I just stared at her and tried to communicate with my eyes that I really fucking needed a break right now. It must have worked because I walked away with the beer.

I drove home and changed into my nice clothes, but I was stressed the fuck out the whole way because the speed bumps in my beer odyssey made me run late. I finally showed up to the party and knocked on the door, beer securely in my arms. A teammate I knew of but hadn't yet met in person opened the door.

"Oh hey man, you must be [name redacted]. I'm Josh. I'm the new hammer thrower." I stuck out my hand.

Barring Alzheimer's or a traumatic brain injury, I will go to the grave remembering every single detail about this interaction. He looked at my hand for a full second and made the conscious decision to do absolutely nothing with it. Just left it there hanging. Then he turned up his chin, cocked his head, and stared at a spot that must have been about two inches above my eyes. He curled his upper lip, baring his front teeth in what can only be described as a douche-snarl.

He said exactly four words to me, and there hasn't been a single day since that I haven't thought about them.

REALLY FAGGOT BUSCH LIGHT

"Really, faggot? Busch Light?"

I was floored, for a few reasons.

ONE: The sports world is drowning in toxic masculinity, but if you had called someone a faggot in front of any one of my teammates at Santa Barbara, you would have been chewed the fuck out for being a bigoted piece of shit.

TWO: This guy's need to act like a hard-dicked motherfucker to someone he'd never met took complete precedence over basic human decency. He literally chose to be a hardass instead of a human being. He was denying his very species-hood for the sake of what he perceived to be masculinity.

THREE: He called me a slur whose power is rooted in misogyny, in feminizing men—because of the brand of light beer I drink. I didn't even know that was a thing. Would he have shaken my hand if I'd shown up with a 30 of Bud Light? Or Coors? Or a camelback filled with grain alcohol and jet fuel? Or a goat skin drenched in the blood of my enemies?

To invent a gendered hierarchy of cheap beer brands to reaffirm that you have a big penis and that your dad is proud of you and that you're worthy of being loved was so stupidly pitiable that it made every other variable in the equation seem equally absurd.

It's classic *reductio ad absurdum*: Proving a statement is false by showing its acceptance would be sheer fucking nonsense. If it's absurd that your identity as a man would be dependent on the marketing decisions of a few beer conglomerates, then all the other shit we do to be perceived as masculine or feminine must also be absurd.

Everything became clear in that one moment: It's all bullshit.

I call myself a bro mostly because I think the label and associated images are funny, but also because I vaguely fit the description—I have a large group of male friends, I drink a lot of light beer from a can, I wear backwards hats. But, I don't let it determine the other parts of my life. I identify as a feminist, I have meaningful non-romantic relationships with women, and I read food magazines on planes and shit. It's where all those things intersect that really defines me.

Even though you can choose your identity, it's still perceived and acted on by others. I call myself a bro because I have the agency to do that, and I know everything it encompasses and stands for.

So, what do I know about chicks? They like wine and beer, meat and vegetables, chocolate and Doritos. It's almost as if they're multidimensional people who have complex wants and interests. Crazy.

I titled this chapter "Stuff Chicks Like" mainly for shits and gigs, but also because I wanted a farcical outlet where I could safely admit that I, in fact, often enjoy a roasted cauliflower soup, or a nice bowl of wine-poached cherries, or some festive pumpkin spice crème brûlée.

Most of these recipes are things I happened to cook for girls in the past, whether it was for friends, strangers, girlfriends, family members, girlfriends' family members. But they're also things that I have and would cook for myself or any brochacho on the planet.

Show me one guy who doesn't appreciate a good silky velouté. You can't, because veloutés are the shit.

Cheers.

ROASTED CAULIFLOWER VELOUTÉ

with Gremolata

SERVES 2

Soup

½ head cauliflower, separated into florets

¼ cup vegetable oil

2 slices rye bread

1 cup heavy cream

2 cups chicken stock (or vegetable stock to keep it veg-friendly)

½ teaspoon black pepper

4 sprigs fresh thyme

Salt

2 tablespoons lemon juice

Gremolata

2 cloves garlic, peeled

¼ cup chopped fresh parsley

Grated zest of 1 lemon

1 tablespoon olive oil

2 teaspoons lemon juice

¼ teaspoon black pepper

This is straight out of my Valentine's Day 2014 playbook. Andrea and I had just started dating, and I needed to do something impressive to bribe her to continue dating me. Cooking was the only way to do that, because outside of the kitchen I'm a negligent manchild who can barely function in the world and has nothing of value to offer to another human. So I cooked.

I set up a super-romantic tablescape (I watched a lot of Sandra Lee growing up) decked out with candles, flowers, and a few probably-garbage bottles of wine on my apartment building's rooftop. I prepped out a three-course meal and gave my buddy Ryan detailed instructions on how to plate all the dishes. I even dressed his ass up in a bow tie so he could be our official waiter for the night. I know, right? I'm fucking endearing.

The first course was this roasted cauliflower velouté with gremolata and rye croutons. She swooned. That was followed by braised pork belly with an orange–pinot noir gastrique and a side of pommes Anna. She swooned harder. Then, the fucking coup de grâce: an artfully plated (I put it in the freezer ahead of time so Ryan couldn't fuck it up) sundae with vanilla ice cream, Zinfandel-poached cherries (page 106), and spiced chocolate ganache.

Andrea and I have been together ever since. (I really hope we're still together by the time you read this, because I really don't know what I'd do without her. Like, not even from an emotional standpoint: I drive her car to work every day and we share a cell phone plan and I wouldn't know how to get my own.) But that battle of romantic attrition was won after the first course.

1 For the soup: Preheat your oven to 425°F. Throw the cauliflower in a large mixing bowl, drizzle with the vegetable oil, and toss to coat. Arrange the florets so they're not touching on a large baking sheet and roast for 15 to 20 minutes, until you get a good amount of char on that veg. Always char your veg. Char is good.

2 While that's roasting, toast the slices of rye bread in the oven for about 10 minutes, until toasted, bordering on burnt. Remove and let them hang out on the counter so they can dry out a little bit. These are going to be croutons.

3 Bring the cream and stock to a boil in a large saucepot. Reduce the heat to medium and add your roasted cauliflower, black pepper, and sprigs of thyme; let simmer for 15 minutes.

4 Remove the sprigs of thyme and transfer the liquid to either a food processor or a blender. WARNING: If there's a hole in the top of your blender or food processor, make sure you ball up a kitchen towel and cover it before you turn the machine on. We don't need any scalding accidents today. Add 1 teaspoon salt and buzz that baby up for a few minutes until it's real nice and smooth-like. Put it back in the saucepot and continue to simmer over medium for an additional 5 minutes, until it's the consistency of a bisque, albeit a chunky one. Turn off the heat, add the lemon juice, and any additional salt if you think it's needed.

5 Meanwhile, to make the gremolata: Peel the garlic and mince it as fine as possible. Throw the parsley and lemon zest on that garlic and continue to chop the shit out of it until it looks like a fine paste. Put your gremolata mush into a small bowl, then whisk in the olive oil and lemon juice and add black pepper.

6 Cut the crusts off the dried rye bread and cut the rest of the bread into ½-inch squares.

7 Divide the velouté evenly into a couple of bowls and top with your rye croutons and a super-artistical splooshing of your saucy gremolata.

KALE CAESAR

with Parmesan Frico

SERVES 2

1 cup grated Parmesan cheese

1 bunch curly kale (also known as green kale, also known as normal kale)

2 tablespoons white wine vinegar

1 teaspoon salt

2 cloves garlic, peeled

2 egg yolks

1 tablespoon anchovy paste

1 tablespoon lemon juice

¼ teaspoon black pepper

2 tablespoons olive oil

⅓ cup vegetable oil

A frico is a lacy, stained-glass disc of golden cheese that crunches like the first leaves of autumn and has a roasty umami that just seems to deepen the flavors of all the other ingredients and...BLARGHHHHHHH. Sorry, I just vomited. You put a mound of cheese in the oven, then you wait 10 minutes, and then you have crunchy cheese. There is no single food with a higher impressiveness-to-easiness ratio than the Parmesan frico.

The first time I made this was for my homecoming group junior year of high school. I thought I could kill two birds with one stone by avoiding a pre-dance trip to the Cheesecake Factory while also impressing the shit out of my high school girlfriend's parents. It only half worked. Well, I guess three-quarter worked. I successfully skipped the Cheesecake Factory, and my date's mom was super-impressed, but her dad was old-school and from the South and couldn't stop hitting me with the "real men don't cook" stare.

---

1 Heat your oven to 350°F. On a greased baking sheet, divide the Parm into 4 equal, circular mounds about ¼ inch high. Throw the sheet into the oven for about 12 minutes, or until the Parm rounds have turned a nice golden color and appear to be solid discs. Let them cool for 10 minutes. Gently remove the cheese Frisbees and reserve.

2 Oooooh, you get to massage kale. This is exciting. I'm excited for you. This is one of the most exciting things you can do with kale. Top three, easy. Use a paring knife to slice the leaves away from the ribs, then throw the shitty, woody ribs away. Give the kale a rough chop to leave 1-inch shreds. Drizzle with a tablespoon of vinegar and ½ teaspoon salt, then use your hands to mash at it haphazardly for 3 minutes. Just like you would massage your romantic partner.

3 Mince your garlic as finely as humanly possible. Unlike massaging, put some real effort in here. Drop it in a large bowl with the egg yolks, anchovy paste, lemon juice, the remaining 1 tablespoon vinegar, the remaining ½ teaspoon salt, and the pepper. Whisk! Then, slowly stream in the olive oil, whisking the whole way, and then ditto for the veggie oil. This is called Caesar dressing. It's a dope thing to know how to make.

4 **Toss your kale in the dressing, then plate:** Form the kale into a mound. Mounds are rad. Crumble some of your Parmesan frico on top. That's it. That's all a salad should be. No croutons—putting bread in a salad makes it a sandwich.

BURRATA
with
Charred Tomatoes
& Parsley

SERVES 4

2 tablespoons lemon juice

1 tablespoon white wine vinegar

Salt

A few cracks of black pepper

1 tablespoon olive oil

¾ cup roughly chopped fresh parsley

1 small shallot, thinly sliced

2 tablespoons vegetable oil

12 ounces cherry or grape tomatoes

2 orbs burrata (about 8 ounces total)

¼ cup toasted pine nuts

4 slices grilled crusty bread

You can be a dick and scoff at trendy ingredients. Or you can use them to your advantage and piggy-back on their brief moment at the cool-kid table. I suggest you do the latter. Burrata—an orb of gooey stracciatella di bufala surrounded by a mozzarella skin—is having a fucking moment right now. And by all means, it's a deserved moment. There's something incredibly satisfying about breaking through that outer cheese membrane and watching its liquidy viscera pour out all over the plate. But this recipe isn't limited to burrata.

Ten years ago these blistery tomatoes would have been slapped with a fat slab of chèvre, and ten years from now there's going to be a new trendy cheese. Who knows what it's going to be: Sheep ricotta? Smoked pig gouda? Maybe global warming will wreak havoc on our traditional farming practices and we'll have to start milking house pets for dairy. Anyways, when the time comes, finish the dish with a wedge of cat cotija or something.

1 Whisk together the lemon juice, vinegar, ½ teaspoon salt, and pepper in a tiny, adorable bowl. Slowly stream in the olive oil while continuing to whisk. Toss half of that dressing with the parsley and shallot in a bowl and reserve the rest for later drizzling.

2 Heat a large sauté pan on the highest heat setting you feel comfortable with. Make it hot. And make it nasty. Drop, drop, drop the vegetable oil into the pan. When it starts to smoke, throw in the cherry tomatoes and vigorously (add extra vigor if you'd like) sauté them for about 1 minute, until charred and starting to blister on the outside. Turn off the heat, sprinkle with some salt, and toss to coat.

3 Plate your cherry tomatoes first. Make them into a loose mound or something. I don't know. This is stupid anyways. Then put a blob of buratta on top. Put the green parsley stuff on it afterwards. Garnish with toasted pine nuts sprinkled around all aloof-like along with a drizzle of the dressing.

4 Serve with slices of toasted bread. Boom.

BURRATA WITH
CHARRED TOMATOES
& PARSLEY, *page 100*

SEARED
SALMON
with
Shiitake Broth

SERVES 2

1 (1-pound) skin-on Atlantic salmon fillet

2 tablespoons vegetable oil

Salt

8 ounces shiitake mushrooms

2 tablespoons butter

2 cups chicken stock

¼ cup chopped fresh parsley

¼ cup chopped fresh chives

2 tablespoons lemon juice

¼ teaspoon black pepper

This is still the best hero ball I've ever played, and this dish right here is my co-MVP. Well, a much drunker and shittier version of this dish. But let's not let facts get in the way of a good story. It was the first house party of the year, and one of my roommates invited a girl over whom he'd had a crush on for a long time. Because I am a good person, I decided to sacrifice my own good time to wingman. Sometimes you gotta be a team player. He was terrible with girls and talking, and with being a genuinely interesting human being, so she got bored late in the night. After she mentioned leaving to get pizza, sometime around 3 a.m., my roommate shot me a panicked look. His chance at love was about to be buried in the dirt by fucking Domino's, which is a special kind of cruel fate. So I pulled what I consider one of my most clutch friend moves of all time, pulled out a few salmon fillets, some mushrooms that I got at a local organic produce co-op, and went to town cooking the two of them the weirdest drunk food dinner of their lives. She left after that and he still never got anywhere with her, so technically this dish has a zero percent batting average, but I tried goddammit, and no one can tell me otherwise.

1   Divide the salmon into two equal fillets. Or make yours bigger. Since you're doing the cutting, you can very easily make that happen.

2   Heat 1 tablespoon of the oil in a large sauté pan on medium-high high heat (between medium-high and high). Meanwhile, liberally season both sides of your salmon with salt. When the oil starts to shimmer, throw down your salmon skin-side up. You always want to make sure the skin is the last thing you cook so it can be as crispy as possible. I saw some chef on TV say that once when I was a kid, and now I judge the fuck out of anyone who cooks skin-side down first. Fucking losers.

3   Sear for about 3 minutes on the flesh side, then flip and continue searing for an additional 3 minutes on the skin side. Make sure that the skin is nice and crispy and a little bit burnt. Burnt is good. Take the salmon out of the pan and let it rest on a cutting board.

4   While the fish is resting, trim the stems from the shiitakes and clean the dirt off of them with a moist paper towel.

5   Heat the remaining 1 tablespoon oil in a large sauté pan on medium-high high heat (between medium-high and high; this should seem familiar). Sear off your shiitake mushrooms for about 2 minutes on one side, then flip and sear for another 2 minutes on the other side.

6   When the mushrooms are all toasty and roasty, add the butter. Let the butter melt, then add the stock. Mix it together and let it cook down for 5 minutes, until the liquid is reduced by half.

7   Stir in the parsley, chives, lemon juice, ½ teaspoon salt, and the pepper. Continue to cook another 2 minutes.

8   Place the salmon skin-side up in shallow bowls. Pour the mushroom broth around it, making sure the skin never gets wet.

WHITE ZINFANDEL-POACHED CHERRIES 'N' CRÈME

SERVES 4

'N' Crème

1 pint heavy whipping cream

3 tablespoons sugar

1 teaspoon ground cinnamon

Cherries

1 orange

1 lemon

2-inch knob fresh ginger

½ cup sugar

2 cinnamon sticks

1 bottle ($3.99 or under) white Zinfandel

As many cherries as you feel like eating (12 ounces should do)

Cooking with wine makes you seem worldly and sophisticated—almost as worldly and sophisticated as someone who spent a six-week summer semester abroad in Italy. And that's pretty goddamned worldly and sophisticated. These poached cherries are a very easy way to cook with wine because there are zero opportunities to fuck up. You aren't making a bordelaise sauce where you have to emulsify bone marrow into cabernet; you're dumping fruit and sugar into a vat of cheap, already-sugary wine, then disguising it all with a bunch of sugary cream. This is an absolute soft ball, and you better hit that fat pitch out of the park.

1 **For the 'n' crème:** Combine the cream, sugar, and ground cinnamon in a food processor. Press the "go" button on it. Process for about 2 minutes, until the cream becomes whipped. This is called "whipped cream." I don't normally say this, but: The stuff you can make at home is way better than the stuff out of the can.

2 **For the cherries:** Slice the orange and lemon into rings. Cool. You're off to a fantastic start. I'm proud of you.

3 Peel the ginger. You can do this with a vegetable peeler, or, if you're confident in yourself, a paring knife. You can also scrape the edge of a spoon against it and it peels pretty fast. Just make it have less skin. No skin, even. Slice that ginger knob in half lengthwise.

4 Throw all the non-cherry stuff—the citrus fruits, ginger, sugar, cinnamon sticks, and wine—all of that, into a medium saucepot. Turn the burner on high.

5 Meanwhile, pit those cherries. If you have a cherry pitter, throw it away and slap yourself in the face for having a cherry pitter. Grab a chopstick or a chopstick-shaped stick, push it directly through the top of the cherry (the butthole), and forcibly stab the pit through the bottom part of the cherry (also the butthole; cherries have two buttholes).

6 Stir your pot of stuff with a wooden spoon. Let it come to a boil and keep it running, stirring occasionally, for about 6 minutes, or until reduced by half. Remove the cinnamon sticks and citrus and other floaty bits of stuff. Your cheap-ass wine should be infused with flavors now, making the fact that it is, indeed, cheap-ass wine a non-issue. Ever want to disguise flavors, throw other flavors at it. Write that down.

7 Drop the heat to medium. Add your cherries and let them hang out in the slightly simmering wine for 2 minutes. Remove the cherries and put them in a bowl.

8 Keep the pan on medium and reduce the wine for another 3 minutes or so, just until it turns nice and syrupy. Throw the cherries back into the wine and let it cool before serving.

9 Put cherries in a bowl with some of the wine soup. Put whipped cream on top. Smear all over your body. Run through the streets.

KABOCHA SQUASH BROSOTTO

SERVES 3 TO 4

1 medium kabocha squash

3 tablespoons butter

1 small shallot, minced

2 cloves garlic, minced

1 quart chicken stock

1 cup Arborio rice (or any rice that doesn't end in "A-Roni")

1 teaspoon finely chopped fresh sage leaves

¼ cup grated pecorino cheese

Salt

½ teaspoon black pepper

The simplest way to impress someone is with confusion. Dazzle them with bullshit and all that. You want to be that asshole at the party who talks people up about music and intentionally drops names of artists that no one could have ever possibly heard of, then acts surprised that you haven't heard of them because they're, like, super-big in the underground Icelandic house scene. "Oh, you haven't heard of kabocha?" you might say, quite impressively. "Yeah, I mean, you've probably just heard it referred to as Japanese pumpkin," you would continue, increasing levels of impressiveness oozing from your mouth-hole after each word. But really, kabocha is sweeter than butternut squash and doesn't have that farty bacterial taste, and it's a fantastic ingredient that you should start using ASAP. It's like a fudgy sweet potato. Fuck. I love kabocha.

---

1 Peel and halve the kabocha squash. This is an annoying process and it involves you hacking at the skin with a knife for like 10 minutes and digging out the gross-ass seeds from the middle with a spoon. But it's worth it. Do you want to impress people or not? Dice up half that kabocha into ½-inch cubes and save the other half for…I don't know, whatever else people do with kabocha squash.

2 Heat a large sauté pan on medium heat and add the butter. When the butter is melted and smelling like you wanna lick the pan (don't do it, man), throw in the shallot, garlic, and kabocha. Sauté on medium for about 6 minutes, until the squash starts to tenderize. You're going to leave the kabocha in the pan while you make the risotto. It's a super-starchy squash, so it holds up to longer cooking methods really well and gets super-fudgy and sweet. It's fucking lovely.

3 Heat the stock in a medium saucepan on high on a separate burner. When it comes to a boil, turn the heat to low and let it hang out.

4 Toss the rice and sage into the sauté pan with the squash and turn the heat up to medium-high. Stir the rice with a wooden spoon and sauté for 3 minutes. You want to coat the rice in some of that excess fat.

5 **This is the annoying part:** Add that hot stock ½ cup at a time and continue to stir the mixture until all the liquid is evaporated. Repeat this over and over and over until all your stock is gone. The rice will soak up ½ cup of stock every 2 to 3 minutes, making the whole process take about 25 minutes or so.

6 When you've added the last of your stock, add half the cheese and turn off the heat after about 30 seconds of stirring, before all the stock is completely absorbed. You want the risotto to still have a good amount of excess liquid when you serve it. Season with salt and pepper, and garnish with the rest of your cheese.

CREPES
with Bananas Fireball

SERVES 6

Crepes

1¼ cups whole milk

2 eggs

1 tablespoon vegetable oil

1 cup flour

1 tablespoon granulated sugar

½ teaspoon salt

Butter, for the pan

Bananas Fireball

½ stick (4 tablespoons) butter

½ cup granulated sugar

¼ cup dark brown sugar

3 bananas, sliced into coins

½ cup bullshit cinnamon-flavored whiskey

WARNING: This recipe is supposed to impress people. Sometimes it has the opposite effect. Sometimes it makes you look like an unhinged monster driven by fire lust and people will refuse to get near you for fear that you will sacrifice them to Balrog, demon of the flame. And by sometimes, I mean literally the only time I've ever made it. So I'm batting a thousand on that.

My roommates and I were tailgating before a UCLA night game, and we were having so much fun fucking around in the parking lot that we decided not to go into the stadium. We made that into a habit. It was generally a smart decision. That day, we ran into a group of girls who did the same thing.

We made friends, we drank beers, and we played a heated game of one-hand beer football before one of them announced she was hungry. Which was impeccable timing, because I just happened to have all the ingredients for Bananas Fireball on deck. (Not 100 percent sure why I brought bananas, butter, and sugar to a tailgate, but I did, and I regret nothing. Except for what happened next. But not really.)

I slapped a cast-iron pan on the grill, threw down a pat of butter and some sugar, and tried to act as impressive as possible. The girls were impressed. My roommates were impressed. It was all very impressive, and that was even before the impressive part happened.

The bananas went into the pan, they got sautéed, and then out came Fireball—the sickly sweet, cinnamon-flavored whiskey that took sorority houses by storm in 2013. I started slashing liquor at the grill and flames shot into the sky.

Things got out of hand. My roommates and I took turns to see who could create the biggest fire tornado. We fell into a paganistic trance, wild-eyed and fueled by Natty Light, the primal essence of flame, and the need to impress the opposite sex.

Apparently our all-male fire orgy freaked the girls out, because we turned around and they had all left. Oh well. More Bananas Fireball for us.

1 I guess you should make your crepes first. That would make sense. Whisk all the stuff except for the butter in a bowl until it's smooth. Technically you're supposed to let crepe batter rest in the fridge so it can...do something. But we're not very technical around here.

2 Heat a large sauté pan on medium-high heat. Add about a teaspoon of butter—just enough to fully coat the pan. When the butter melts, ladle in about ¼ cup of your crepe batter, then pick up the pan and rotate it in a circular fashion until the batter is evenly dispersed.

3 Let the batter cook for about 60 seconds on one side, until it's dry on the top and golden on the bottom, then use the thinnest spatula you have to gently and carefully and not-fuck-uppedly flip it. Continue to cook for another 30 seconds on the other side, or until golden and toasty, then remove from the pan. Repeat until you have a bunch of crepes.

4 Now, for the liquored bananas: Heat a sauté pan on medium-high and add the ½ stick of butter. When it melts, add both sugars. Stir that together for about a minute, then add the banana coins.

5 This is the dangerous part, except that it's only dangerous if you're a dumb asshole. And you're not a dumb asshole (fingers crossed). Pour the whiskey into the pan, then gently tip the pan towards the stove's flame. If you only have an electric stove, use one of those long BBQ lighters to ignite the bananas. There is going to be a large flame—don't get scared! That's just your food becoming more impressive. (If anything gets out of hand, you can just clamp a lid down on the pot to suffocate the flame. Do NOT throw water on it unless you're trying to look like Aaron Eckhart in *The Dark Knight* for the rest of your life.)

6 When the fire naturally extinguishes itself, put together the dessert: Fold a crepe into quarters to form a little rounded triangle and pour some of those alcoholic 'nanners on top.

Fuck it: I love pumpkin spice. I love everything about it. I love the taste, I love the fanfare, and I even love the inexplicably intense public vitriol about it. (Like the voice of our generation, Rico Richie, said, "If you ain't got no haters, you ain't poppin'.") Call me basic—I'm done giving a shit. You know what, you're basic for calling me basic: The only thing more basic than blindly loving trends is blindly hating trends. If you take away all the loaded cultural implications of pumpkin spice, you're just left with a delicious mixture of ground cinnamon, ginger, clove, nutmeg, and allspice. And that shit's great with everything, especially crème brûlée.

PUMPKIN-SPICE-LATTE
CRÈME BRÛLÉE

SERVES 4

3 egg yolks

1 cup sugar

1 pint heavy cream

6 tablespoons brewed espresso (cooled down a bit)

3 tablespoons pumpkin pie spice

Bunch of hot water

1   Preheat your oven to 325°F. Whisk together the egg yolks with ⅔ cup of the sugar in a large mixing bowl until the combo looks all nice and creamy. This does something. I don't know what. But definitely something.

2   Heat the cream, espresso, and 2 tablespoons of the pumpkin pie spice in a small saucepot over medium heat until it reaches Jacuzzi temperature. Imagine bathing yourself in it. Ladling it all over your naked body. You should be able to do that comfortably.

3   Stream the hot-tub-hot cream into your sugary egg yolk stuff really slowly, whisking the whole way through.

4   Divide the mixture evenly among 4 ramekins, then place those in the bottom of a large casserole dish. Pour hot water (also Jacuzzi-hot) into the baking pan itself until it comes about halfway up the ramekins.

5   Throw the casserole dish in the oven for 40 to 45 minutes. Ehhhh, take it out after that. It's probably good. Only you would know though. Like, I'm not there, so...You should be able to jiggle the pan and see the middle of the custards move. If they're super-stiff, you know you've gone too far and the custard has overcooked.

6   In a small mixing bowl, whisk together the remaining ⅓ cup sugar and the remaining 1 tablespoon pumpkin pie spice. Sprinkle it evenly over the tops of your custards.

7   Light up a blowtorch. I wish I had any safety tips, but I don't. Probably just google "how to not die using a blowtorch." That's what I did, and I'm not dead yet. If you don't have a blowtorch, find a friend who does drugs. They always have blowtorches. Or you could pop the brûlées under the broiler for a minute or two. But blowtorches are so fun. Torch the sugary pumpkin spice mixture on top, moving the flame back and forth and around so it cooks evenly. Get some good char on top—don't be afraid to push the limits of burningness.

8   Serve during peak PSL season (late April through mid-February).

STRUGGLE Snax

THE
STRUGGLE
Is Real

▶ If you cook beef jerky in beer for a long enough time at a low enough temperature, it almost starts to resemble *ropa vieja*. Or at least that's what you tell yourself to avoid the crushing shame that comes from eating dried beef sheets rehydrated in cheap liquor for dinner.

And it's reasonable to feel you have to justify it. You imagine what others—family members, trusted mentors, high-ranking religious officials if that's your jam—might say about your dietary choices, and none of it is good.

"This is morally reprehensible and in direct opposition to all tenets of *kashrut*," Grand Rabbi Abramowitz would say (you're Jewish in this hypothetical; just go with it).

"You should really take better care of your body," says fictional JV tennis coach Steve, who knew you had a big serve and all the talent in the world, but goddammit, Scherer, you don't listen to nobody and also he doesn't exist. "I thought you were smarter than this."

"You have an effeminate body type and poor personal hygiene," says Jerry. Not sure who Jerry is.

With all due apologies to nonexistent and incredibly judgmental people—go collectively fuck yourselves. We all do what we have to do to get by, and sometimes that involves binge-eating ramen and discount lunch meat, or making an entire dinner out of some old carrots and a box of bootleg-ass Rice-A-Roni, or throwing candy bars in a blender with water and protein powder just to get some calories in you. The struggle comes in many forms.

When I first moved to L.A., I couldn't figure out how to scrape up food on a regular basis. There were no grocery stores within a mile of my apartment, I didn't have a car, everything was too hilly to skate, and I have an impressively low tolerance for walking. I also wasn't about to drop coin on meal kits or delivery Thai food every night because I was in the middle of accruing a modest $30,000 in student debt. My main source of nutrients was the Chevron mini-mart a convenient 200 feet from my apartment.

It started with late-night coffee and ham sandwiches when I had to get a bunch of work done—or maybe some Diet Mountain Dew and a microwavable chimichanga if I was feeling froggy. After a while, I knew all the cashiers' names, and they knew mine, provided I was cool with my name being "Hoss," "Boss," or "Big Man." (While we're on the subject, "Hoss" is easily the coolest name in that set.) I felt more at home shopping there than I did going to an actual grocery store, and I was spending about $2.79 per calorie-dense feasting session, which is damn near unbeatable.

Obviously there are severe limitations on what kinds of foods you're going to find at a place that mainly sells gasoline, cigarettes, lotto tickets, and energy drinks. But there are a surprising number of options there. They always had an ample supply of hard-boiled eggs, and if you hoarded some pico de gallo and mayonnaise from the hot dog condiment bar, you could make a pretty solid egg salad sandwich on one of their fresh-baked (at some point in time it was fresh-baked) croissants.

If you needed to add some healthy complete protein to your dinner, you could stop by the Chevron and pick up a jar of Tostitos bean dip, and maybe even an apple for dessert. Look at you being all healthy! A warning on the apples though: There's a really ominous "THIS FRUIT HAS NOT BEEN PRE-WASHED" sign, which I'm assuming they had to put there because something terrible happened in the past; I think their apples have a straight-up body count.

The one thing that makes shopping at gas stations, liquor stores, mini-marts, bodegas, or corner stores, or whatever else you want to call them, so fantastic is the complete and utter lack of judgment. No one there gives a shit what you do because they've seen everything. Nothing can faze them anymore.

I watched a homeless guy run into the Chevron once, grab a whole tray of Mentos, walk up to the register with his hand in his pocket like he had a weapon, and scream in the cashier's face, "I'll fucking kill you, bitch," as loud as he could before sprinting out the door while knocking a few shelves over.

The dude who calls me "Big Hoss" didn't even flinch. It was like this homeless dude wasn't even there. Like he was just background noise on the same level as the whirring of the rolling hot dog machine or the occasional shuffling of ice in the fountain drink dispenser.

I'm standing there completely fucking slack-jawed because I thought I was going to see a stabbing, and then Hoss Guy cashier pulls the most Hoss move of all time and just goes, "Next in line, please."

When shit like that happens on a daily basis, so much so that it's completely normalized for Hoss Guy, then you going in there to buy condoms and cigarettes and rolling papers and malt liquor and Doritos and running a bag of beef jerky under the nacho cheese dispenser for an unsettling amount of time is nothing. Hoss Guy probably welcomes your weird shit with open arms compared to the general population of people he has to deal with.

You don't get that same experience at a big chain store. You ever try to buy condoms at a grocery store? Multiple times I've seen parents shield their kids' eyes walking past me, and multiple times cashiers have said something to the effect of, "Looks like you're about to have a fun night" and then make eye contact for an extended period of time.

I moved away from that Chevron awhile ago, but now I live less than a quarter mile away from a Bob's Liquor Mart, which—if you'll allow me to brag for a second—has an objectively impressive grocery section for a liquor store.

Most of the canned goods have been expired for more than three years and the produce never gets changed out and one time their dairy fridge broke for four days and they just kept on selling that warm milk. It might be my favorite grocery store in L.A.

The cashier there calls me "Boss Man." It's not as good as "Big Hoss," but it'll do.

HOW TO
SHOP AT A
Gas
Station

———

This guide is by no means meant to be dogmatic. My intention is not to draw a hard line on what you should or shouldn't do with your money; I just want to gently steer you towards making informed choices. Are convenience store apples a universally good decision? Not even a little bit. Do I still buy them because life is difficult and your morals need to be flexible to accommodate that? Damn straight.

FIVE THINGS YOU SHOULD
Always Buy

- -

1

SUSHI

Weren't expecting that one, were you? Artificial crab—an apocalypse-proof mixture of compressed whitefish, salt, sugar, and fake-but-delicious crab liquid—rolled up with rice is one of the safest decisions you could make at a gas station. Load that shit up with soy sauce and neon green, burning goo (calling it wasabi would be a stretch), and enjoy your lunch while the rest of the world looks at you with disgust.

- -

2

MEXICAN SNACK CAKES

This might be a regional thing, but if you're ever in California, find the Mexican snack cake with the most colorful packaging, buy six, and crush them ASAP. The best one is Gansito—it's a Twinkie, plus strawberry jelly, covered in a chocolate shell. Where else are you going to get quality and innovation like that?

FIVE THINGS YOU SHOULD
Never Buy

3
40S

I could be wrong on this, but I think it's illegal to sell 40s of malt liquor outside of a gas station.

4
CONDOMS

Sure, they're cheaper at a big-name pharmacy, but condoms are still inexplicably frightening to purchase in public, and gas stations are a safe space.

5
SLUSHIES

Similarly to giant bottles of malt liquor, proper frozen carbonated sugar bombs are almost exclusively limited to gas stations and convenience stores. Aim for the most brightly colored flavor. Just as a poison dart frog's flamboyant colors signify poison, a slushie's flamboyant colors signify deliciousness.

1
FRESH FRUIT

I can understand it if you're a busy parent stopping for coffee on the way to work, and you need to grab your kid a snack that won't give him diabetes. But holy shit, in any other circumstance, why would you even go near the moldy apples in the basket by the cash register? On a hot day, you can actually smell them fermenting in real time. But on the flip side, you might be able to get drunk off them...

2
EGGS

There is a 100 percent chance that anyone you see buying the individually packaged hard-boiled eggs from a gas station is a sociopath.

3
UNFLAVORED COFFEE

Come on, man, live a little. You can get shitty plain coffee anywhere, but where else are you gonna find Almond Joy creamer and Thin Mint Salted Caramel What-the-Fuck-Ever Hazelnut Folgers on tap?

4
HOT DOGS (AFTER 3 P.M.)

First of all, you have to admire the ingenuity of those heated metal rollie-machines whose only function is to keep dick-shaped foods slightly above lukewarm. Second of all, you'd have to be insane to think that the employees are ever tossing old dogs for new ones. If you show up at midnight, and there's still a hot dog rolling around, it's been there for at least 12 hours, maybe 15. Maybe even a few days. Maybe that hot dog has been there since day one, since prehistory, since the primordial ooze. Maybe time is a flat circle, and this eternal hot dog is its focal point. Either way—gross.

5
PRETZELS

This is not limited to gas stations. Pretzels should not be purchased or consumed anywhere. They are the Ned Flanders of snack foods. If you're dying of starvation on a desert island, and there are only pretzels around, eat a handful, then pray to the struggle snack god for the clouds to burst open and rain Doritos.

CHORIZO RAJAS TACOS

MAKES 12 TACOS

3 large fresh poblano peppers

½ white onion, minced

¼ cup chopped cilantro

1 teaspoon vegetable oil

1 (12-ounce) tube of the cheapest fresh chorizo you can find (shouldn't cost more than $1.50)

½ teaspoon salt

¼ teaspoon black pepper

1½ cups whole milk

12 corn tortillas

2 limes (if you can afford them)

Atheist God bless you, chorizo. You are undoubtedly the cheapest, most calorie- and flavor-rich tube of meat-like product at the supermarket, and this is why you have forever been a staple in my fridge. I'd say don't look at the ingredients, but I always advocate staring the grosser things in life right in the face. Don't shy away from the lymph nodes, salivary glands, and cheek fat—the only three representations of pork in the Cacique variety of chorizo, aka the only brand you should be buying—rather, embrace them.

This is struggle food at its most base level: taking the parts of the animal that no one else wants and turning them into some dope-ass tacos. *Rajas con crema* is a typical Mexican dish made with sautéed poblano peppers simmered in cream, and it was one of my staple orders at La Super-Rica—yeah, the taqueria that Julia Child lost her shit over. It's also a great way to get rid of that milk spoiling in the back of the fridge.

---

1 Remove the stem and seeds (no seeds, no stems, no sticks!) from the poblanos, then cut each pepper into ¼-inch-thick strips. Also, at this point you might as well mix the onion and cilantro in a bowl and leave it somewhere. I don't know. Just makes sense.

2 Heat the vegetable oil over medium-high heat in a large sauté pan, and when it starts to shimmer, throw in the large chorizo turd. Break it up with a spoon and stir it around until it's cooked most of the way through—about 5 minutes—and has bled its delicious chorizo fat.

3 Throw in your poblano strips, drop the heat to medium, and cook until the peppers are tender, about 10 minutes. Season with salt and pepper, then pour in the milk. Normally this recipe would use heavy cream, but that shit's mad expensive, and you don't have any money, and when the water evaporates out of milk—as it would in a hot pan—it literally turns into heavy cream.

4 Continue to stir the sausage and milk and pepper concoction until all liquid evaporates out and you're left with a violently orange, flavored mush.

5 Figure out a way to heat the tortillas. I'm normally a dry hot pan kind of guy, but sometimes I like to take stacks of three, wrap them in a damp paper towel, and microwave them for like 20 seconds. Mmmm, steamed using science.

6 Scoop some sausage goo into each tortilla, garnish with onion and cilantro, maybe a squeeze of lime if you can afford it, and then shove in your facehole.

SMOTHERED
DINO
NUGGETS

SERVES 4

1 large white onion

2 tablespoons butter

1 (32-ounce) box Dino Buddies brand dinosaur-shaped chicken nuggets

¾ cup mayonnaise

¼ cup ketchup

2 tablespoons finely chopped pickles or pickle relish

1 teaspoon Worcestershire

1 teaspoon Sriracha (or whatever hot sauce)

6 slices American cheese (the gross kind)

For the uninitiated, Dino Nuggets are like normal chicken nuggets except they're vaguely shaped like prehistoric lizard monsters. They were also a staple on Sizzler's kids' buffet in the late '90s. The price at the time was $6.99 for adults (my dad) and $.99 for kids under 10 (me and my brother). When my older brother's neck beard grew suspiciously not-10-years-old-looking, he would hide in the bathroom when my dad ordered, and he'd sneak to the table when the Texas Toast dropped.

Cheating Sizzler out of $6—which would pay for a whole month of my federally subsidized elementary school lunches—during every graduation and birthday meal between 1998 and 2001 is how I realized that food could be a source of hardship. That it can be joy and shame wrapped in the same package. Those endless vats of dino nugs were my OG struggle food. They were at the same time celebratory and a crushing reminder that we weren't like the other rich families in Orange County. But they were fucking delicious. Smother them in cheese.

1 Take your big-ass onion and dice it as fine as you can. This is going to do a couple of things: (1) speed up the caramelizing process; and (2) mimic the cut of In-N-Out onions and remind you of the times you weren't too poor to eat out.

2 Heat the butter in a large sauté pan over medium heat and, when melted, add the onions. Stir sporadically but vigorously—vigor is the secret ingredient, not love—for 20 minutes, or until the onions are brown and caramelized-ish.

3 Make your dino nuggets not-frozen. This goal could be accomplished using many implements—oven, deep fryer, microwave, sous vide bath, dumpster fire—but, for the greatest combination of convenience and preservation of dignity (microwaves are for Top Ramen and Top Ramen only), preheat your oven to 400°F. Line a large baking sheet with foil for easy cleanup purposes, then dump out all the frozen chicken products on there, spreading out so as to not overlap and create unnecessary steam. Throw in the oven for 20 minutes.

4 While your nugs are probably burning, stir together the mayo, ketchup, pickles, Worcestershire, and hot sauce. Is it the best Thousand Island? No. Do you really want to put in the work to make it better? Didn't think so.

5 When the prehistoric-shaped pressed and formed chicken products are warm, assemble them in a large pile still on the baking sheet. Place the slices of cheese over them like a squishy neon yellow blanket. Mash your caramelized onions on top of the cheese in a smooth layer, then pop back in the oven for an additional 5 minutes, or until the cheese is melted. Splash your Thousand Island over the top in the most artistic pattern you can muster—go real Jackson Pollock on this motherfucker—then feast like the fat, princely asshole you were meant to be.

SMOTHERED DINO NUGGETS,
page 119

BACON-WRAPPED BANH MI DOGS

MAKES 4 DOGS

2 large carrots

1 (1-pound) daikon (use like 8 normal radishes if you can't find daikon) (This will make way more pickles than you need, but they keep for at least 2 months in the fridge, and you'll be glad to have them on hand.)

1½ cups white vinegar

¼ cup sugar

1 teaspoon salt

4 thin slices bacon (cheapest you can find)

4 hot dogs (cheapest you can find)

1 tablespoon vegetable oil

4 hot dog buns (cheapest you can find)

1 jalapeño

½ medium white onion

4 sprigs cilantro

¼ cup mayo

Sriracha to taste

This one is a little bit of a conundrum. Banh mi—and we're talking about legit Vietnamese banh mi, not the gentrified-ass hipster variety—generally costs about $2.75 per 9-inch sandwich. They are buy-two, get-one-free for the Grand Opening event that's been going on for at least three years at my local joint, but I guess everyone can't bank on extended celebration prices. So why crank the struggle meter up on a dish that's already mad cheap and meant to be a quick working-class lunch? Because hot dogs! Actual banh mi ingredients like pork liver pâté and headcheese can be hard to find. But what's a hot dog if nothing more than an Americanized version of the Vietnamese pork roll, *cha lua*? Yaddadamean?

---

1 Get the carrots and daikon in some brine. Since you're just slapping them on a hot dog, don't worry about them not pickling for too long—as long as they sit in brine for at least an hour, you're totally fine: Peel the carrots and daikon, cut into matchsticks, then throw into some sort of Tupperware container or something. Heat up 1½ cups water with the vinegar, sugar, and salt over high heat in a saucepan, and when it comes to a boil, pour it over the vegetables. Throw in the freezer for a couple of minutes to speed up the cooling process, then put them in the fridge.

2 Wrap one strip of bacon around each hot dog and secure in place with toothpicks at each end. Heat the vegetable oil on medium heat in a large sauté pan and, when the oil starts to shimmer, throw down your hot dogs. Cook until the bacon is crisp and all that delicious fat has melted through your hot dogs. Place the dogs on paper towels to drain.

3 Toast the hot dog buns. Or not. It doesn't matter. You just do you. Slice the jalapeño into rings, slice the onion into thin strips, and trim the ends off the cilantro sprigs so mainly just the leaves remain.

4 Spread some mayo on each side of each bun, place a bacon-wrapped meat tube in each, then throw down some drained carrot and daikon pickle, a few shards of jalapeño and onion, and some cilantro, then absolutely douse that shit in Sriracha. Because why not?

FRIED BOLOGNA & KIMCHI
REUBENS

MAKES 4 SANDWICHES

½ cup mayonnaise

¼ cup ketchup

1 tablespoon Sriracha

¼ cup minced scallions

1 (14.5-ounce) can sauerkraut

4 ounces kimchi

16 ounces real shitty bologna

Vegetable oil

8 slices of the cheapest rye bread you can find

8 slices fake-ass Americanized Swiss cheese (the plastic-wrapped square kind)

There are few things in this world I'm above eating, but lunch meats that cost less than a dollar per pound are generally in that category. Food shouldn't be that cheap. You can't physically raise an animal and process it down for that price—there's gotta be a catch somewhere in the equation. Maybe it's pink slime; maybe the meat's cut with wood pulp and MSG; maybe it's egregious workers' rights violations at the factory. It's likely a combination of all three.

But when you come home drunk from a party and find a stack of bologna coins that your roommate bought on manager's special, what are you going to do? Not eat them? That'd be stupid. Plus, the blood is off your hands at that point. You had no active role in buying the emulsified garbage meat—you just wandered up to a fridge and found it. Anyways, the best way to cook the stink off questionable animal by-product discs is to fry the shit out of them and then cover the whole mess in cheese and fermented ingredients. That's like the first rule of cooking. Also, if you call it a Reuben, and you're drunk enough, you can convince yourself that you're eating real food.

1 Stir together the mayo, ketchup, Sriracha, and scallions in a mixing bowl. This is a janky-ass version of Russian dressing. And I mean, like, reallll janky. But, the freshness of the scallions is really going to cut through all the fatty cheese and meat and fermented cabbage. Also, fuck you, don't judge me.

2 Drain off the liquid from the sauerkraut, and ditto for the kimchi. Run your knife through the kimchi to cut it into rough strips, then mix that in a bowl with the kraut. Save for later.

3 **Fry the shit out of that bologna until it's edible:** Heat 1 teaspoon oil in a large sauté pan over high heat until the oil shimmers and smokes. Throw down 4 slices of bologna in each go-round, and make sure you put some real color on there. You know the way you hard-sear a steak? (Sure you do.) Do that to each slice of bologna. Something something Maillard reaction or whatever. When the discs of processed meat are nice and crispy, remove and let drain on some paper towels. Go ahead and fry the rest in more oil.

4 **Assemble the sandwiches.** Or just give up and walk away. I guess those are the two options you really have. Either one works on my end. Assuming you want to eat though, take a slice of bread, spread on some jank-ass Russian, top with 4 slices of fried bologna, 2 slices of Americanized Swiss cheese, ¼ cup of your mixed fermented cabbage, and some more hefty splooshes of that pink Russian sauce, then top it off with another bread hat. Repeat to make a total of 4 sandwiches.

Recipe Continues

5 Now, how do you melt the cheese and get everything else to at least a pleasant lukewarmness? That's a hell of a fucking question, son. You got yourself a few good options:

A **PAN:** You do this just like a grilled cheese. Fry in butter over medium heat, flip when the bread is toasted, and repeat.

B **OVEN:** Split each sandwich in half—bologna and one slice of cheese on one side, fermented cabbage and cheese on the other—then throw that in the oven to melt before reassembling.

C **PANINI PRESS:** I don't know, maybe a distant relative bought you one for your birthday like six years ago? Maybe you worked at a Jersey Mike's and stole a sandwich press out of spite when they fired you for vaping in the walk-in? I don't know your life, but if for whatever reason you have a panini press, now would be the time to employ it.

D **WAFFLE. FUCKING. IRON.:** If the options are ever "waffle" or "don't waffle"...you know what to do.

RAMEN SPAM CARBONARA

SERVES 4

1 teaspoon vegetable oil

6 ounces SPAM, diced into small cubes

2 large eggs

¼ cup Parmesan cheese (don't shy away from the green plastic bottle kind), plus more for serving

Cracked black pepper

4 packages chicken-flavor instant ramen

Salt

All the best foods are portmanteaus. Cronuts. Ramenburgers. Sushirritos. But before we can go on to the next frontier of mashing words together—pizzaroni 'n' cheese, moussakachos, tikka masalasadas?—we need to pay our respects to the OG: *SPAM*. It's a clever combination of the words "spiced" and "ham," because the one thing always missing from ham was that big punch of spice in the back of your tonsils. But, where SPAM really beats out normal, comparatively low-tech nitrate-cured pork products is shelf life.

The first move you should make when stocking a new kitchen from scratch is to buy at least a half dozen cans of SPAM, then bury them in the deepest corner of your deepest cabinet. They become like little sodium-enriched Easter eggs that you're going to find when you least expect it. And unexpected SPAM is the best kind of SPAM.

Surprise SPAM, already great for snacking on plain, is also useful in making traditional recipes with hard-to-find ingredients. Want to make pasta carbonara but can't find guanciale, aka cured pork jowl? Surprise SPAM is there for you. This recipe follows a rather pure carbonara formula—salty pork, plus cheese, plus raw egg, plus noodles—but it gets a self-deprecating twist with instant ramen.

1   Heat the vegetable oil in a large sauté pan over medium-high heat. When the oil starts to shimmer and move freely in the pan, add the SPAM and cook until crisp, 5 or 6 minutes. Turn off the heat and reserve.

2   In a large mixing bowl, whisk together the eggs, Parm, a few cracks of black pepper, and two of the seasoning packets from the ramen. You're going to want that chicken flavor (aka straight-up MSG) in there. Set aside.

3   Bring a quart of water to a boil in a medium saucepot. Salt the water liberally, then drop in noodles from all four packages and cook for 2 minutes, until just under al dente. (OK, so I know it's *instant* ramen and can't really be al dente, but fucking humor me here.) Drain the noodles and reserve 1 cup of the noodle water.

4   Crank the heat of the SPAM pan on high and, when the frankenpork starts to sizzle, throw in your noodles and toss to coat. When coated in pork fat, add the noodle water.

5   Now, this is real important, so listen the fuck up. You're going to turn off the heat of the pan, then transfer all the contents over to that bowl of eggs and stuff and then toss it violently. Like, real violently, real fast. You know the movie *2 Fast 2 Furious*? Yeah, like that, but with convenience food. If you don't toss all the shit together fast enough, the eggs are going to scramble, and you don't want that. You want this shit silken.

6   Let the noodles sit for 2 minutes to absorb the sauce, then throw them on a plate and garnish with more cheese and pepper. Maybe if you have something green you can throw it on there too? I don't know.

RAMEN SPAM CARBONARA,
page 127

BBQ-BEEF-STICK PIZZA BAGELS

SERVES 4

- 4 store-bought bagels (quality not an issue)
- 1 cup BBQ sauce (store brand is best)
- 1 cup shredded mozzarella cheese
- 1 Slim Jim Sasquatch Big Stick (the best kind)
- ½ red onion, thinly sliced
- 1 small jalapeño, thinly sliced
- 3 sprigs cilantro, for garnish

I eat dried and processed meat products like it's my fucking job. In high school (and college, and now...), I pretty much lived with a constant stream of beef jerky and diet energy drinks entering and exiting my body. It was so bad that my high school girlfriend refused to get in my car because all the old jerky wrappers made it smell like someone set off a Slim Jim–based dirty bomb in the ventilation system. Though I've recently tried to cut back on the habit—aside from the money issue and the general grotesqueness, the bowel obstruction was a factor—there's still something about the smell of a freshly popped bag of jerky, or summer sausage, or beef stick, or Mexican-brand pickled sausage that gets me all riled up. Tap into their culinary potential and ride the lightning.

1　Preheat your oven to 375°F. Slice all the bagels in half across the equator (doing it the other way would be stupid), then evenly distribute the BBQ sauce across each bagel half and top with the mozzarella.

2　Slice the beef stick thin, then spread the slices, super-artistic-like, across the sauced-up, cheesed-up bagels. Do the same with the onion and jalapeño—but be extra artistic with it.

3　Throw them bad boys in the oven for 10 minutes, or until the cheese is melted and the bagels are crispy. Garnish with cilantro and feel free to squirt a bunch more BBQ sauce at it. Maybe some squiggles or something. People love squiggles.

OK, OK, OK, I'm not gonna bullshit you—these aren't even close to beignets. But, in my defense, I don't actually know what a beignet is other than some Francophilic bullshit name applied to fried dough covered in borderline-irresponsible amounts of powdered sugar. And that's pretty much what this is. Plus, throwing some French stank on it makes you feel way better about battering and frying what is essentially a mangled child's sandwich. Shame and self-loathing aside, it's way easier than actually making dough from scratch—aka a total fucking nightmare—and it'll satisfy any and all of the most struggle-ass late-night munchies.

JANKY-ASS
FLUFFERNUTTER
BEIGNETS

MAKES 4 JANKY-ASS BEIGNETS

2 cups vegetable oil, for frying

8 slices cheap-ass white bread

¼ cup milk

2 eggs

2 tablespoons flour

½ cup peanut butter

1 cup marshmallow fluff

½ cup powdered sugar

1 Heat the vegetable oil in a sauté pan over medium-high heat. Cut the crusts off all the slices of bread. Then eat them. No wasted calories here.

2 Whisk together the milk, eggs, and flour in a large mixing bowl.

3 Take four slices of bread and evenly distribute the peanut butter and marshmallow fluff among them, trying to stay close to the center of each slice. Take the remaining bread slices and place them on top of the others. You know, like a sandwich. You've done this before.

4 Pinch the edges of the sandwiches together real hard—if you're using cheap enough white bread, it should create a nice seal—then dip each sandwich into the loose batter you made. Forcibly mash some more batter at the edges to create an even tighter seal. This will help you not die when frying.

5 **Fry that shit, son!** Take the sandwiches—ahem, *beignets,* because French words up the value of anything you put into your body—straight out of the batter bath and throw them in the hot oil, working two at a time, so as not to overcrowd the pan. Make sure the beignets don't touch in the oil. Fry for about 2 minutes on each side, until golden brown, then let drain on paper towels. Dust with powdered sugar and eat before letting them cool because you're not a pussy. (Lol, jk: Totally let them cool; don't be dumb.)

Tacos

> ▶ I grew up on white-people tacos. Well, I grew up on white-people everything because my parents were super-white. If you're not familiar with white-people tacos, they are generally served DIY-style on the dining room table with the ingredients in mismatched Tupperwares and there are never any serving utensils because of course there aren't.

The fillings may include but are not limited to: chunky ground beef sautéed with a Lawry's taco seasoning packet, iceberg lettuce, tomatoes, cheddar cheese, sour cream (healthy whites are using Greek yogurt now), a jar of Pace picante sauce (still the best jarred salsa in the game), and a can of sliced olives that will never get touched and no one even knows who bought them or opened the can but somehow they're always there. Also, scallions. No one eats those either.

I have long rejected the white-people taco. I've lived within a 90-mile radius of L.A. for pretty much my entire life, which means I've always been adjacent to America's—maybe even the world's—best non-white-people tacos. Legit spit-roasted *al pastor* from a truck that parks at a gas station, carnitas braised in its own lard in a copper pot that's been in the same family for generations, tortillas made from organic blue corn imported from Mexico, *carne asada* that's grilled over mesquite charcoal the exact same way they do it in Sonora. I'm drowning in some of the best tacos that history has ever had to offer, and I eat them as often as possible.

But I'm not about to pretend that I could come close to re-creating any of them, let alone pretend that I can instruct you how to do it. So I won't.

If you want great carnitas or *birria de chivo* or *pescado zarandeado* or *frijoles charros,* you get it from someone who's devoted a good portion of their life to making those dishes. If you don't live in an area that has dope-ass Mexican food (lol, sucks to suck), and you have your heart set on making authentic *chorizo verde* from scratch, find someone on the Internet who has some real claim to authority and pretty please ask them.

So, why the fuck do I have an entire chapter of a book devoted to tacos if I can't tell you how to make them? Now you're asking the right questions. I have since learned to embrace the white-people taco, but in a completely different way and on completely different terms than actual tacos. Let me explain.

I've always loved Chipotle. It's relatively cheap, it's convenient, you get your food in two minutes, and it's just flavorful enough to incentivize you to keep eating it. Someone once called my Chipotle fandom into question, asking why I didn't instead patronize many of the local mom-and-pop burrito establishments. At first, I was mad at myself. Shit, why *don't* I go to local spots? I mean I *do* go to local spots all the time—I fucks with *machaca* burritos like it's no one's business—but why would I ever neglect them for Chipotle? Because Chipotle doesn't make burritos. Chipotle makes wraps.

A little white-people history for you: Sometime back in the late '80s probably—the cultural zenith of white people—whites discovered a thin, pliable, edible food wrapper called a flour tortilla. They didn't know what to do with it so they stuffed it full of white-people shit—lunch meat turkey, muenster cheese, Dijon mustard, arugula, hummus—and called it a wrap.

Barely seasoned white rice, simply grilled chicken, lettuce—yeah, Chipotle is out there making wraps. And they do them better than anyone. A Chipotle wrap could never go toe-to-toe with a legit Jerez-style *burrito de guisado,* but no one should be putting them in the same category anyways. I've learned to appreciate white-people burritos for what they are, and the same goes for white-people tacos.

A Crunchwrap Supreme (technically still a taco) from Taco Bell is never going to come close to the pure, erotic, porcine pleasure of the best carnitas, but there's room in your heart to love both. You can love the gooey, violently yellow cheese pouring out of Taco Bell's tortilla labyrinths without sacrificing your appreciation for legit Mexican food.

Those are the types of tacos that I'm going to teach you how to make, because those are the tacos that I understand on a deep level. Love the classic white-people combination of chicken, bacon, and ranch dressing? Let's figure out how to wrap that in an easy-to-transport tortilla. In the mood for some braised short ribs but all your utensils are dirty? Use a tortilla as edible gloves, grab a handful of shredded meat, and shove it all in your mouth-hole.

If it would make you more comfortable, you can call them mini-wraps instead of tacos. But something about a rose, and smelling, and other names and all that.

SHORT RIB
DOUBLE-DECKER
TACOS

MAKES 12 TACOS

2 tablespoons vegetable oil

3 pounds bone-in English-cut short ribs

Salt

1 large white onion, roughly chopped

3 large carrots, roughly chopped

24 ounces (2 bottles) brown ale

2 (15-ounce) cans white beans

2 tablespoons olive oil

1 cup sour cream

2 tablespoons prepared horseradish

1 teaspoon lemon juice

Black pepper

12 taco-size flour tortillas

12 crunchy taco shells (I use Old El Paso's Stand 'n Stuff)

1 bunch wild arugula

8 ounces Gruyère cheese, shredded

The most interesting thing white people have done to the taco is to try to re-architecture the tortilla to fit their white-taco sensibilities. To white people, tacos are crunchy, but crunchy taco shells are small and break easily, which is how the giant taco salad in a fried tortilla bowl exists.

Now, white-people-facing taco companies are coming out with new innovations like crunchy taco boats and crunchy taco shells that stand up as you fill them. They're fun to make fun of, but even more fun to cook with. I wanted to shed any faux-Latin pretense of your typical white-person taco and go with full on white-people ingredients like arugula and horseradish. White people love arugula.

1 Preheat your oven to 300°F. Heat a large, heavy-bottomed sauté pan (hopefully cast iron) on high heat with the vegetable oil. Season up the short ribs with a whoooooole lot of salt and, when the pan's hot, sear them off for 3 minutes per side, all around. Work in batches. When they're all seared, transfer to a deep casserole dish.

2 In the same sauté pan, add the onion and carrots, then deglaze the pan with that brown ale, scraping at the bottom of the pan with a wooden spoon to get the tasty bits. Add 2 cups water and 1 teaspoon salt and bring to a boil. Then carefully pour that mixture over the short ribs. Cover the casserole with tin foil and throw in the 300-degree oven for at least 4 hours, until the ribs are falling off the bone.

3 Remove the short ribs from the braising liquid and let cool a bit. When they are cool enough to work with, shred with a fork and put in a large mixing bowl. Splash about 2 cups of the fatty braising liquid in there and add salt to taste.

4 Drain the beans in a colander and rinse them with cold water to get the can stink off them. Puree the beans in a food processor with the olive oil. Transfer the puree to a pan and heat on medium, just to warm it through; reserve.

5 Whisk together the sour cream, horseradish, and lemon juice and add a few cracks of black pepper. Reserve that too.

6 Heat the tortillas in groups of three in a large skillet on high heat, just until they're a little toasty. For each taco, spread about a tablespoon of bean puree evenly over a tortilla, then fold that around a crunchy taco shell. Spoon some of your braised short ribs into the taco shell, then top that with wild arugula, some of your horseradish sour cream, and shredded Gruyère.

THE
CBR
(CHICKEN BACON RANCH)
TACO

MAKES 6 TACOS

6 strips bacon

1 pound boneless skinless chicken thighs

3 tablespoons Cajun seasoning mix

1 teaspoon salt

3 tablespoons vegetable oil

1 cup bottled ranch dressing

¼ cup hot sauce

6 taco-size flour tortillas

8 ounces shredded sharp cheddar cheese

½ head iceberg lettuce, shredded

2 Roma tomatoes, diced

1 avocado, sliced

This is an essential combination of foods that hits on the same flavor notes as a good club sandwich, but instead of white bread it is in a tortilla and it also has hot sauce ranch on it. Those are all improvements. There is no culinary technique involved in this recipe, nor is there anything you have to think very hard about. You have chicken. You have salty pig parts. You have bottled salad dressing. Lean in to how easy and delicious this is.

---

1   Heat the oven to 375°F. Throw the bacon strips down on a baking sheet, then toss it in the oven. Check back in 15 minutes, then flip and cook another 5 minutes, until crisp. Let the bacon drain on a bed of paper towels.

2   If there's any extra fat on the chicken thighs, trim it off. Throw the chicken thighs into a big mixing bowl and season with the Cajun spice blend and salt. Pour 2 tablespoons of the vegetable oil on there and mash it all up with your hands.

3   Heat the remaining 1 tablespoon vegetable oil in a large sauté pan on high heat. When it's screaming hot, add the chicken thighs, working in batches so as not to crowd the pan. Don't be afraid to press on the chicken with a spatula to make sure all the surface area is getting seared properly. After about 5 minutes, flip the thighs over, and sear for another 5 minutes. When they're browned and cooked through, pull them out of the pan, dice them up into little bits, and reserve.

4   Whisk together the ranch dressing and hot sauce. Boom. Sauced.

5   Heat the tortillas in groups of three in a large sauté pan. When the first side is all toasty and warm, flip the tortilla, then add a small handful of cheddar. You really want that cheese to melt on the tortilla.

6   Place the tortilla on a plate and put some chicken on top of that cheesy flour disc, then add a strip of bacon, then some shredded lettuce, some tomatoes, and an avocado slice or two. Then drown that whole motherfucker in your hot-sauced ranch.

PORK SCHNITZEL TACOS

with
Fennel & Apple Slaw

MAKES 6 TACOS

Brussels Sprouts

15 Brussels sprouts

2 tablespoons vegetable oil

Salt

Black pepper

Fennel & Apple Slaw

2 fennel bulbs

½ red onion

1 Granny Smith apple

3 Thai chilies

2 tablespoons white vinegar

1 teaspoon Dijon mustard

1 teaspoon lemon juice

1 teaspoon honey

1 teaspoon mayonnaise

Salt

Black pepper

2 tablespoons olive oil

I have a theory that has yet to be proved wrong, insofar as you can prove an opinion wrong: Every dish tastes better in a tortilla. I don't even mean that hyperbolically, like when people say, "Everything's better deep-fried!" Yeah? You ever gotten drunk and deep-fried a bunch of grapes? Because I have, and it's fucking weird. But, I can't think of even one hypothetical that would be worse in a tortilla. Coq au vin? Fuck yeah, call it a coq au taco. Pork schnitzel with fried Brussels sprouts and fennel apple slaw? Huh. I don't know, I've never thought about that.

---

1 For the sprouts: Heat your oven to 425°F. Slice the Brussels sprouts in half lengthwise, coat in the vegetable oil, and season with salt and pepper. Put on a baking sheet and roast, flipping halfway through, for about 25 minutes, until there's some good char on both sides, but the sprouts aren't too mushy. Turn off the oven, but keep those little fart grenades in there to keep warm.

2 Meanwhile, make the slaw: Trim the fronds off each fennel bulb and discard the outermost layer of the bulb. Slice off the woody butthole area, then slice it as thin as humanly possible. Please, just go buy a mandoline for this. Slice the red onion really thin as well. Take that apple, core it, and cut it into very, very thin slices. Then cut those thin slices into thin matchsticks. Put all of it (the fennel, onion, and apple) in a mixing bowl.

3 Mince the Thai chilies and throw them in a small bowl along with the vinegar, mustard, lemon juice, honey, and mayo, then whisk. Add ¼ teaspoon salt and a few cracks of black pepper. Keep whisking as you slowly stream in the olive oil.

4 Dress the slaw with the dressing and toss to coat. Don't use all the dressing though. Use as much as you see fit.

Schnitzel

1½ pounds boneless thin-cut pork chops

2 cups flour

2 eggs

1 cup whole milk

2 cups plain breadcrumbs

Salt

Vegetable oil, for frying

Black pepper

6 corn tortillas

5 **For the schnitzel:** Wrap those pork chops in plastic wrap, then lovingly beat the shit out of them with a blunt object until they're paper thin—no more than ½ inch thick. Honestly, I just use my fist most of the time. I find it actually works better than a meat mallet, and almost as well as an empty wine bottle.

6 Get out three mixing bowls. In the first, put the flour. In the second, whisk the eggs and milk together. In the third, combine the breadcrumbs and 1 tablespoon salt.

7 Heat about an inch of vegetable oil in a large sauté pan on medium-high heat. Season up the pork chops with salt and pepper. Dredge them in flour, then in the egg wash, then in the breadcrumbs, really making sure to pack on the breadcrumbs.

8 Pan-fry the chops for about 4 minutes each side, or until golden brown and cooked through. Work in batches so the chops are never overlapping and have ample room to fry. You can likely go two at a time at least. Let them drain on a paper towel before cutting them into strips.

9 Heat up the corn tortillas in the microwave or on the stovetop. Throw down some schnitzel strips, then a few roasted Brussels sprouts, and then some of that sweet, funky slaw.

SCALLOP
DYNAMITE
TOSTADAS

MAKES 6 TOSTADAS

12 ounces bay scallops

4 ounces white mushrooms, finely chopped

½ white onion, thinly sliced

1½ cups mayonnaise

¼ cup Sriracha

1 bunch scallions

6 tostada shells

2 tablespoons furikake

I am a big fan of cheap sushi. I mean, I'm talking the real bottom-of-the-barrel-type shit. One of my go-to lunches in high school was a Cheeseburger Big Bite and a California Roll from 7-Eleven. Just give me cold rice, soy sauce, and something dead that once lived in the ocean, and it scratches the sushi itch that I need it to. (I also think there's something inherently prejudiced about admonishing cheap sushi but idolizing cheap tacos. We'll save that one for another day though.) The key is to not get too ambitious with it. Stick to spicy tuna and mayonnaise-y crab bases, maybe getting some eel or salmon if you grow to trust the place. But if you're looking to splurge and look like a big baller, get a $9.95 Dynamite Roll. It's a California roll topped with a bunch of crustacean meat that's been drowned in Sriracha, and then the whole thing gets thrown under the broiler until the mayonnaise brûlées and the Cali roll is nice and sweaty. This recipe cuts out the middleman and makes it into a tostada so you can get to that sweet burnt mayo fish more efficiently.

1 Preheat your broiler to high. Dry the scallops with paper towels so they don't leak excess liquid. Place the scallops in a mixing bowl along with the mushrooms and onions.

2 Whisk together the mayonnaise and Sriracha, then pour that sweet, sweet orange mayo over the scallops and toss to coat. It should be realllll mayonnaise-y. Like, disgustingly so. But don't worry, that's the sweet spot.

3 Dump all of that into any sort of baking sheet or ovenproof vessel, and throw it under the broiler for about 5 minutes. The key here is to get the mayonnaise good and burnt while cooking the scallops and 'shrooms to a perfect medium rare.

4 Slice the scallions vertically as thin as possible. Yeah, vertically. I know, right? Make a bowl of ice water, then dump the scallions in the ice water and let soak for about 3 minutes. They should curl up into a cool scallion nest. They look rad. Dry them off by blotting firmly with a paper towel before using.

5 Lay down a tostada shell, top it with some of that scallop 'n' mayo slop, a little nest of scallions, and then dust it with furikake.

SENEGALESE
LAMB &
PEANUT STEW
TACOS

MAKES 12 TACOS

½ cup vegetable oil

2 pounds lamb stew meat (or get lamb leg steaks and cut them into 1-inch pieces yourself)

Salt

1 large white onion, diced

2 cups canned tomato puree

1 cup organic smooth peanut butter (not the stuff that was on your sandwich as a kid)

3 tablespoons Maggi seasoning sauce (most major grocery stores have it in their "ethnic" aisle, but if you can't find it, substitute soy sauce)

2 teaspoons white pepper

1 teaspoon cumin

1 habanero, sliced in half

2 russet potatoes

12 corn tortillas

½ red onion, thinly sliced

Sprigs of cilantro, for garnish

Every time we flew from California to Pennsylvania to see my dad's side of the family, my cousin Hawa would send us back home with gallons of frozen stew that we stashed away in our carry-ons. The dish is called *mafé* and it's super-popular all over West Africa, but Hawa grew up in Senegal, so, fuck it, I'm throwing Senegal in the recipe title.

She would always serve it over rice, but when I was a kid, I didn't know how to make rice—I still barely know how to make rice—so I got weird with it. I'd microwave some Ore-Ida and make mafé Tater Tots, or scramble up some eggs for a mafé omelet. But the number one application for me has always been the mafé taco. Mafé nachos are a close second though. If you have leftovers, you know what to do.

1 In a big, heavy-bottomed stockpot—the biggest you've got—heat the vegetable oil on high heat. Season the lamb liberally with salt, then brown off the pieces in the oil, turning often.

2 Throw in the onions and continue to sauté until the onions have sweated. Next, add the tomato puree, peanut butter, Maggi seasoning, white pepper, and cumin. Stir to combine everything, add a teaspoon of salt, then dump in a quart of water and continue to stir until everything is combined.

3 Turn the heat to medium, add the habanero, and let the mixture cook down for about 2 hours. Don't cover it, because you want it to reduce, but use a splatter guard if you have one.

4 After 2 hours, peel the potatoes, dice into ½-inch cubes, and throw them into the stew. Simmer for another 1 hour, then taste and adjust the salt level if it needs it. If the sauce has become too thick and pasty, add water. Too thin, crank the heat and continue to reduce.

5 Griddle up some corn tortillas, drop some fall-apart tender lamb and potatoes in the center, then top with red onion and fresh cilantro.

PORK BELLY
TACOS
with Fish Sauce Caramel

MAKES 12 TACOS

Pork Belly

1 (3-pound) slab of boneless skinless pork belly

Salt

Black pepper

Daikon Pickle

1 cup rice vinegar

2 cups sugar

1 teaspoon salt

1 medium daikon

Fish Sauce Caramel

2 tablespoons lime juice

2 cups sugar

½ cup fish sauce

1 habanero, sliced

3 star anise pods

1 cinnamon stick

Tacos

Vegetable oil, for shallow frying

12 corn tortillas

1 bunch fresh mint

1 bunch fresh basil

3 Fresno chilies, thinly sliced

¼ cup crushed peanuts

WATCH OUT

THIS IS AN
OVERNIGHT
RECIPE

If I were in a cooking death-match and my life depended on one dish, I would make these tacos. I pitched that idea to Food Network by the way, and they didn't love it. Their loss. It has literally every single thing that I love about food in it. The fat on the pork belly is so rendered that it melts right to goo. The meat cubes are still crispy from their post-braise oil bath, even after being slathered in that fermented umami-bomb caramel sauce. Pickled daikon for crunch and acid, mint and basil for herbaceousness, Fresnos for heat, and peanuts because I like putting peanuts on stuff. The flavors would be too intense without the tortilla, but the plain starchiness absorbs just the right amount of funk from everything else. Every other recipe in this book is garbage compared to this.

1 **For the pork belly:** Preheat your oven to 300°F. Season the pork belly liberally with salt and pepper, place it in a large casserole dish with 2 cups water, cover tightly with foil, and throw in the oven. Braise for at least 6 hours, until fork tender. Take the pork belly out of the braising pan and chill it in the fridge overnight.

2 **That same night, you should also pickle that daikon:** Mix ½ cup water, the rice vinegar, sugar, and salt in a saucepot on high heat and whisk until the sugar dissolves. When it comes to a boil, turn off the burner. Peel the daikon, then cut it into matchsticks as thin as possible. Place the daikon in a heat-proof container, pour the pickling liquid over it, and let it chill in the fridge.

3 **FAST-FORWARD TO ONE DAY LATER and make your fish sauce caramel:** Heat a heavy-bottomed saucepan on medium-high and combine ¼ cup of water, the lime juice, and the sugar. Let that cook for about 15 minutes without fucking with it. If you stir prematurely, the sugar will crystallize on you. Take it off the heat when it's a deep reddish brown, then carefully whisk in the fish sauce plus an additional ¼ cup water. Place it back on the heat for about 2 minutes and stir it all together, then pour into a heat-proof jar. Throw in your sliced habanero, star anise, and cinnamon and let it steep.

4 **To assemble the tacos:** Take out your chilled pork belly and cut it into 1-inch cubes. In a large sauté pan, heat 1 inch vegetable oil over medium-high heat. When the oil is all shimmering like a goddamned fool, add your pork belly cubes. The goal here is just to get them a little bit crispy and render some additional fat. Use a wooden spoon to ladle oil over the top of the belly cubes, then, when they're nice and golden brown, about 3 minutes, remove and drain on some paper towels.

5 Put the belly meats into a large mixing bowl then drizzle a bunch of that fish sauce caramel over the top. Toss until every piece of pork is sufficiently and fully lacquered.

6 Heat up some corn tortillas on a griddle, and then you're ready to plate. Top the tortillas with some pork belly, some pickled daikon, a few mint leaves, a few basil leaves, some sliced Fresno chilie, and finish it all off with some crushed peanuts.

PORK BELLY TACOS
WITH FISH SAUCE
CARAMEL, *page 147*

OXTAIL
HEXAGONAL TORTILLA PRODUCT

MAKES 6 TACOS

👉

Recipe Continues

Taco Bell's Crunchwrap Supreme is the second most important fast-food item of all time, just behind the Doritos Locos Taco, and just in front of McDonald's Fruit 'n Yogurt Parfait. I'm telling you, man, McYogurt is fantastic.

The Crunchwrap completely shattered the lock on Pandora's box. If you look at every Taco Bell item pre-Crunchwrap Supreme, it has an analog in legit Mexican cuisine. Their crunchy tacos are modeled after *tacos dorados,* their gorditas are *tacos Arabes* (even though a gordita is already a real dish, but let's not split hairs), and their Mexican Pizza is pretty much a *mulita.*

But the hexagonally folded tortilla with a tostada membrane separating hot and cold ingredients was an absolute stroke of original genius. In my incredibly professional and expert opinion, this was the dish that paved the way for every future Taco Bell innovation. There's no DLT without the Crunchwrap.

This recipe isn't so much an elevation as it is an homage. There might be oxtails and little gem lettuce in there, but I tried to stay true to the Taco Bell color scheme (violent yellow and deep brown) and flavor profile (pure sex).

Oxtails

3 pounds oxtails

Salt

36 ounces (3 cans) beer of your choice

2 tablespoons cumin

2 tablespoons chili powder

2 tablespoons cocoa powder

1 tablespoon onion powder

1 tablespoon garlic powder

1 tablespoon paprika

½ tablespoon black pepper

Nacho Cheese Sauce

1½ cups whole milk

8 ounces quality American cheese, shredded

4 ounces sharp cheddar cheese, shredded

2 tablespoons pickled jalapeño juice

1 teaspoon turmeric

1 **For the oxtails:** Preheat your oven to 300°F. (You could also use a slow cooker for this part, but it's going to be harder to drain off the fat.) Liberally season the oxtails with salt, line them up along the bottom of a casserole dish, then pour the beer and 2 cups water all over them. Cover tightly with foil, put in the oven, and braise for at least 6 hours. But really, the more you can let it go, the better. You need all that collagen to leach out of the bones and make your braise nice and goopy.

2 When the braise is done, remove the oxtails and place in a Tupperware in the fridge to use later. Pour all the leftover liquid into some sort of more vertical container. I use my giant measuring cup. Pop the container in the freezer for about 2 hours, after which you can scrape all the fat off the top and just be left with pure gelatinous essence of beef.

3 Pour the defatted liquid into a saucepot on medium heat. Break down all your oxtail meat and then give it a good mincing with your knife. You want this to have almost no meat texture to it. Just unrepentant beef goo, straight to the dome. Stir the oxtail meat into the braising liquid, then add all your spices and season up with salt. Continue to reduce the mixture for another 5 minutes to incorporate all the flavors. The final texture you're going for is almost a meat-rich gravy. There should be a good amount of liquid, so add more water if you have to. Throw the oxtail goop in the freezer to set up while you prep everything else.

TURN THE PAGE FOR ASSEMBLY INSTRUCTIONS

Tacos

6 large burrito-size flour tortillas
  (very important that they are
  burrito size)

6 crunchy tostada shells

Shredded baby gem lettuce

Diced Roma tomato

Sour cream

4 For the nacho cheese sauce: In a medium saucepot, heat up the milk over medium heat. Add the American cheese, cheddar, pickled jalapeño juice, turmeric (tastes like yellow!), and ½ teaspoon salt. Whisk until everything is all whisked and stuff, then turn off the heat.

5 For the tacos: Heat up a sauté pan on high heat—or a big-ass griddle if you have one, that'd be rad—and heat the tortillas for just a few seconds on each side to make them more pliable. Put a few tablespoons of now-cold oxtail goo in the center of a tortilla, then top that with a little bit of nacho cheese sauce. Throw a tostada shell on top of that, then hit it with your lettuce, tomatoes, and sour cream.

6 Now for the tricky part: the hexagonal fold. First, make sure your pan is still hot, because after folding, you need to sear this off ASAP, Rocky. Start by grabbing any edge of the tortilla and folding it in towards the middle. Then, take the next available edge next to the one you just folded over and repeat the process to make five total folds. It's actually pretty intuitive.

7 Once the folds are complete, keep your hands pinching it shut, and then slam it on the griddle, folded-side down. Sear for 30 seconds, and then cook for another 45 seconds on the bottom side to make sure the oxtail heats.

8 Fuckin' get at it, man. Right now. Also, be careful, because hot oxtail liquid will squirt out and get you in the face.

HOW TO

Assemble

the Oxtail Hexagonal Tortilla Product

———

1

2

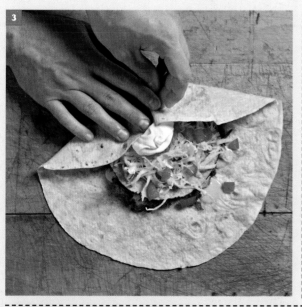

Meat & Fire

▶ There is nothing more American than showing up at an empty parking lot at 6:30 a.m., cracking open a beer, roasting large cuts of meat over fire, then watching a combined three tons of armored humans beat the shit out of each other on a field for your own selfish entertainment. You could drape yourself in an American flag poncho, or train a bald eagle to retrieve cans of PBR, or fly a fighter jet that spells out the complete lyrics to "Free Bird" in the sky, but those all seem hard. Except the poncho thing. You should get a poncho.

Some of the happiest moments of my life have been spent outside the Rose Bowl, drunk and sunburnt and drenched in meat sweats. I've been consistently going to UCLA home football games since I was 15 years old, which means I have my shit on lock at this point. Insofar as your shit can be on lock when your foot is bleeding because you sliced it on a recently shotgunned beer can. But whatever. Here's what you need to know for your next tailgating adventure.

The Food

Large. Cuts. Of. Meat. That's all you need. It's both because large cuts of meat are great, and also because it's incredibly convenient. If you take a few whole tri-tips—or some big-ass ribeyes, or a few pounds of skirt steak, or whole chicken quarters, or pork chops—and marinate them the night before, all you have to do is throw them on the grill, get some char on them, and all the work is done. My favorite strategy even cuts out the useless middleman of plates— grab an industrial-sized bag of tortillas, slice up your meats, and make everything into a taco. It helps if you have one vegetable on hand—some shredded cabbage, or cilantro and onions—and a bottle of hot sauce. Oh, get a bunch of chips too, preferably large bags of the most aggressively flavored Doritos. And a family-sized box of Oreos, or Oreo-adjacent cookies. You gotta have the sweet with the savory.

The Drinks

There are three different drink bases to cover: light alcohol, heavy alcohol, and no alcohol.

I know, I know, what's the point of having nonalcoholic beverages at a tailgate? Because dehydration is real, man. Don't try to be a hardass and end up passing out in the stadium— I've seen it happen. Get several gallons of Gatorade and/or a few 12-packs of Diet Coke. Cool, you'll be OK.

Now for the light alcohol— you need something you can consistently drink over the course of several hours without getting unintelligibly drunk. The easy answer is a whole lot of drinkable, canned beer. You pop a few 30-racks into a giant cooler full of ice and you can drink for days. However, don't rule out orange juice and cheap-ass champagne, hard cider, Mike's Hard, or Smirnoff Ice. Anyone who says that Smirnoff Ice isn't objectively delicious is a goddamned liar.

Heavy alcohol! You need to

have some sort of hard liquor option, in case you need a quick blood alcohol content (BAC) boost because you forgot to drink while you were cooking large cuts of meat. Anything cheap and in a plastic handle works, but Southern Comfort has been a tailgating staple of mine for years. Don't try to get cute and make cocktails either—that always ends up being way more work than reward. The less you work, the more you can fuck around and drink.

The Equipment

You need a grill. This is nonnegotiable. The grill is the absolute center of tailgate life. I'll switch back and forth between charcoal and gas, and I'm pretty agnostic about preference—charcoal equals flavor, gas equals convenience. As long as there's fire and a metal grate, you're OK.

You need two large coolers, both filled with tons of ice. One is reserved solely for cases of light beer, and the other for miscellaneous drinks and marinating meat. Just make sure your meat is secured in a Ziploc bag or Tupperware to prevent cross-contamination.

Bring a cutting board, a knife, grill tongs, and a side towel. If you're going with my large cuts of meat plus tortillas formula, those are the only utensils you'll need. Tongs to flip the meat, a knife to cut it, and a towel to prevent unfortunate burns. You will not need plates, but you will need tons of Solo cups, for both casual drinking's sake and for drinking games, which we'll discuss later.

I can't stress this enough, but you really need a large canopy. It's going to be sunny, and it's going to suck if you don't have consistent shade. Also, get more folding chairs than you think you need. They cost like $6 apiece at big chain hardware stores, and they are more than worth the investment. You'll also need two large folding tables—one for food, one for drinking games. And bring a football. Because football.

The Activities

The easiest game is called Drink the Beer. The rules are as follows: (1) Drink the beer. It's great because it's inclusive and everybody wins. It's similar to the game How Much Beer Can You Drink?, but less competitive. The other classic is Beer Pong—the one where you throw balls at cups, not the one with Ping-Pong paddles, which I'm convinced isn't a real thing. Then there's Cornhole—throwing beanbags into holes cut out in wooden slats. This requires you to own a Cornhole set, which I recommend. A recent favorite game of mine has been Beer Football. It's not a very clever name. The rules are simple: You play a game of touch football while holding a beer in one hand and you have to drink from it often. It gets messy, and everyone ends up covered in beer by the end of the game, but that's pretty much a metaphor for life, so you should run with it. There's one final game, and it is easily the best of them all. It's a drinking game, indigenous to the Santa Barbara region, known as Snappa. The rules are many and difficult enough to explain in person, which means they are even more difficult to spell out on paper. I'd recommend a quick Internet search and a study session. Just know that you get to sit down for an extended period of time, you throw dice very high in the air, and you occasionally have to try and catch those dice with one hand. It is a truly beautiful game. It ends when one team scores seven points. I've been part of 15-minute Snappa games where the winning team has to drink a third of a beer, and I've also seen four-hour games where the losing team drank 17 beers. It's gnarly.

The Main Event

In theory, there is a football game going on inside the stadium that you are near. Or maybe it's a basketball game, or maybe you're just tailgating in the parking lot of a neighborhood Walmart, in which case: damn, mad respect. There is absolutely no obligation to attend the event for which you are tailgating. Football is better to watch on TV than it is in the stadium anyways, and you can always find a group of rich old-timers who are streaming the game with a satellite dish at their obscenely complex tailgate setup. Bring them a beer and catch the game if you feel the need to.

KOREAN
SKIRT STEAK
with
Charred Scallions

SERVES 6

¾ cup soy sauce

¼ cup vegetable oil

2 tablespoons rice wine vinegar

1 tablespoon fish sauce

1 teaspoon sesame oil

½ cup sugar

10 Thai Bird's-eye chilies, minced

8 cloves garlic, minced (or
   2 tablespoons bottled minced
   garlic)

2 tablespoons grated fresh ginger

½ teaspoon black pepper

3 pounds skirt steak or flap meat

1 medium white onion, thinly
   sliced

3 bunches scallions

Fresh lime wedges, for serving

Bunch of super-cheap flour
   tortillas, for serving (optional)

Sriracha, for serving

This recipe is easy as shit. This recipe was designed to be easy as shit. This is because most of the time I'm making this, it's in the middle of a giant golf course at the Rose Bowl in Pasadena, and people are drinking and throwing footballs, and every five minutes or so you have to heckle someone wearing the opposite colors as you. So: All you have is one super-janky foldout table that you bought at Target on the way over, and a portable charcoal grill that you put together without a screwdriver because tools are hard. It's far from a controlled environment, so you need to minimize as much risk as possible.

If all you have to do is pull strips of marinated meat out of a bag, sear them super-hot on the grill, and then toss those directly into the mouths of the waiting drunken horde, then there's not much that can go wrong. Sometimes a football will land on the grill though, so keep your head on swivel.

1 In a big mixing bowl, whisk together the soy sauce, oil, vinegar, fish sauce, sesame oil, sugar, chilies, garlic, ginger, and pepper to combine. Throw the skirt steak and onion into the biggest, heaviest possible Ziploc bag you can buy. Pour the marinade over it, scraping out all the flavor bits at the bottom of the bowl. Those are key. Seal the bag and throw in the fridge to marinate for at least 4 hours, but overnight is best.

2 Light your grill on fucking fire. You want to torch these things. Since I'm usually making these outside in a parking lot somewhere, I use an easily transportable charcoal grill. Lugging around a giant propane tank gets annoying; plus, there's something about the way the charcoal and the sugar in the marinade interact that I love. Sweet and smoky.

3 When your grill is dangerously hot, throw down the skirt steaks. You're not going for any sort of medium rareness here—marinated beef cooked rare is always kind of weird to me because it still looks brown and fuck that—so feel free to play around with the amount of char on the outside. They're going to burn quick because of all the sugar, but a little burn is good. Sear for about 4 minutes on each side, then take off the grill and throw on a cutting board.

4 While the steak is taking its obligatory 5-minute resting period, take all your scallions and toss them on the grill, moving them around a bit for 3 minutes, or until pleasantly burnt on the outside. Cut the steak into edible strips (slice across the grain of fat), and squeeze some fresh lime juice on them.

5 Put the steak and scallions in a grilled tortilla, drown it in Sriracha, and go be the outdoor Beer Pong player you were meant to be.

ENERGY DRINK–BRINED CHICKEN WINGS

SERVES 6

1 tablespoon whole black peppercorns

1 tablespoon whole mustard seeds

1 tablespoon whole coriander seeds

2 teaspoons salt

2 bay leaves

1 fresh habanero, cut in half

2 cups warm water

1 (16-ounce) energy drink of your choice

2 tablespoons white vinegar

1 tablespoon soy sauce

3 pounds bone-in chicken wings

Lime wedges

Every flavor profile should be represented. All of them, even the bad ones. Maybe especially the bad ones. You can only appreciate the good if you've had the shit.

I remember going to a fancy restaurant during its fancy soft opening and eating a fancy dessert where all I could taste was weed. I felt like I just ate the most potent edible I'd ever had and I was about to disappear into hyperspace for 12 to 15 hours. I asked the chef what it was and he said it was lemon verbena brown butter. I told him it tasted like my neighbor Carl's edibles. He smiled and was like, "Oh I know, right?" But why? Why did you deliberately make it taste like bong water? Because every flavor profile is important.

Energy drinks, in my professional opinion, are wildly underused in the kitchen. I've learned to love that bitter, medicinal, over-acidulated twang, just like I've learned to love Negronis and the fartiness of brassicas. Energy drink–brined chicken wings are a good gateway.

1 Heat a large sauté pan on medium heat and add the peppercorns, mustard seeds, and coriander seeds. Toast for 3 or 4 minutes, moving them around constantly so as not to fuck up and burn everything.

2 Throw your toasted spices into a large mixing bowl and add the salt, bay leaves, habanero, warm water, energy drink, vinegar, and soy sauce and whisk it all together.

3 Throw the chicken wings into the brine, toss that shit in the fridge, and let them sit for at least 3 hours. But 12 hours should be your max. Any more than that and it's overkill.

4 Take the chicken out of the fridge and rinse in a colander with cold water just to get all the seeds and stuff off. Dry each wing with a paper towel or else they're going to stick to the grill and that would blow.

5 Light up only the outside burners of your grill. I use gas when I'm not all up my own ass about the "oh man, you gotta taste that charcoal flavor," and I try not to be. Gas is just so much easier to control. If you're using charcoal, make sure the coals are only on one side of the grill. Since chicken wings have so much subcutaneous fat that leaks out, grilled chicken wings are super-prone to flare-ups. And especially with the sugar content of these bad boys, they'll burn up real quick.

6 Throw your chicken wings down anywhere on the grill that's not directly over the heat and shut the lid. Let them run for about 15 minutes before flipping them, but check constantly to make sure they're not getting scorched. Move the wings around as you see fit so they cook evenly. It's a chess match, except I suck at chess and I'm good at chicken wings.

7 When the chicken is caramelized, and it has a little bit of char on the outside, and the fat is rendered, and the meat is cooked through—should take 20 to 25 minutes if you're doing it right—pull them off and serve with lime wedges. And some extra energy drinks to get all riled up.

MALT LIQUOR
CHICKEN

SERVES 2 TO 4,
depending on how hungry y'all are

2 tablespoons vegetable oil

1 teaspoon fresh lemon juice

3 cloves garlic, minced

1 teaspoon paprika (not smoked)

½ teaspoon ground cayenne

½ teaspoon dried marjoram

½ teaspoon dried oregano

1 tablespoon salt

1 teaspoon black pepper

1 whole chicken

1 tallboy high-gravity malt liquor

Lime wedges, for serving

I'm sure you've heard of beer can chicken by now. That's old news. It's like, "We get it, you shoved a can of beer up a chicken's b-hole; we're all very impressed. Can we move on with our lives and stop fist-fucking poultry?" Well we can sure move on with our lives, but you're not going to want to stop fist-fucking poultry just yet there, son.

Beer can chicken is out and malt liquor chicken is in. It's the exact same as beer can chicken, except instead of some shitty dad beer, you're using a tallboy of high-gravity malt liquor preferably bought from a 7-Eleven. The higher alcohol content means there will be more excess sugar evaporating out of the can and steaming your bird meat, creating a maltier, sweeter, earthier profile.

Except that's a complete lie and beer can chicken (and malt liquor chicken by association) is mostly a farce because the beer never actually gets up to a high enough temperature to evaporate, and no liquid can escape through the sides of the can, and all that can of beer is doing is absorbing heat and acting as an ice pack to prevent your chicken from cooking.

It's all for show. However! If you know anything about me, you'll know that I'm all for appearances first, logic and reason second. Like, a distant second. What's cooler than seeing a delicious roast chicken with a can of Mickeys or Steel Reserve or Olde English sticking out its b-hole? Very few things. Also, you can recycle the can afterwards, making it an environmentally ethical meal. Everyone wins.

1 Mix the oil, lemon juice, garlic, paprika, cayenne, marjoram, oregano, salt, and pepper in a bowl and then rub it all over your chicken, really making sure to get in the creases as best as possible.

2 Fire up your grill on high heat. If you're using gas, only fire up the outside burners; if you're using charcoal, only place coals on one side of the grill. You want to cook the chicken using only indirect heat. It's just such a big piece of animal flesh that it won't cook if you try and get any direct char on it.

3 Open your can of malt liquor and pour out the first sip for Biggie. Then take a sip yourself. Then jam the can right up the chicken's b-hole. If the chicken isn't big enough, you may have to use scissors to cut the top part of the can off.

4 You can get away with not tying or trussing up the chicken—it's hard and annoying—but, if you only tie one thing, do the back legs. Take about 1 foot of twine, make the legs cross at the ankles, then tie them together in any way you can figure out how to jury-rig it. There's no wrong way. Trim any extra twine that's hanging off.

5 So, here's how you're going to get that chicken to stand up. The bottom of the can and the crossed legs are going to be your only two points of contact on the grill. That means the chicken's center of gravity has to be somewhere in the middle of those two points.

6 Once you find balance by shifting the breast towards or away from the legs, you stand that motherfucker up on the grill away from the flame, put a cover over the top, and let it run for 35 to 40 minutes, until the skin is rendered and the internal temp of the breast reads 155°F. Once you pull the chicken from the heat and let it rest for 10 minutes, the temperature of the breast should read 165°F, which is what you're shooting for. Use tongs to remove the can, then slice up the breast and serve with some lime wedges for spritzing.

RIBEYES
with
Shallot Sriracha
Butter

SERVES 4

1 stick (8 tablespoons) plus
1 tablespoon salted butter

¼ cup minced shallots

1 teaspoon chopped fresh thyme

Cracked black pepper

1 tablespoon Sriracha

2 (16-ounce) ribeyes, roughly
1½ inches thick

Coarse salt

It's always been weird to me that people even think there's a steak that competes with the bone-in ribeye. New York? Overrated trash. Porterhouse? Unevenly cooked trash. Filet? Bougie motherfucking trash. Sirloin? You know what, kind of underrated actually. It's in a different weight class than the ribeye, but sirloin really does pack in a good amount of flavor at its price point. The marbling on a ribeye is superior to any steak, as is its overall muscle composition. The single best bite out of any cow is the deckle—that little meaty fat cap at the top of the steak.

Some of you may be begging to ask the question, then, "Hey, Josh, if you're such a steak elitist, then what the fuck are you doing putting Sriracha on a pristine cut of beef?" I'm glad you asked: Because Sriracha is fantastic. And I don't mean that in the "I have a Sriracha keychain and T-shirt that I got from Urban Outfitters" fanboy kind of way. I mean I have a genuine culinary respect for the sauce. It has the biggest fermenty kick of any hot sauce on the market and there's so much garlic built in there that you don't have to add any to your compound butter.

When the butter melts into the steak, the fermenty dankness, the garlic, the freshness of the thyme, and the sugar from the Sriracha synergize with the natural sweetness of the shallots. I'm not going to bullshit you: Before I tried this recipe for the first time, I thought it was going to be garbage too. So you're in good company there, hypothetical person.

1 To make a proper compound butter, you gotta do it a day—or at least a couple of hours—ahead. Sorry, I know, I suck. God forbid I try and do something nice for you. Melt the 1 tablespoon butter in a small sauté pan over medium-low heat, then add the shallots, thyme, and 1 teaspoon black pepper and stir. Sauté for 5 minutes on medium-low, just until the shallots have softened. The thyme is going to get a little bit roasty and really blend in with the fat, and this is going to make the shallots less offensive tasting. All good things. Take that mixture, put it in a tiny bowl, and pop it in the freezer for 10 minutes.

2 Cut the stick of butter into 8 equally sized squares, throw it in a microwave safe bowl, then nuke it for 10 seconds. It should be soft enough to mix evenly with a spoon. You want it to be the texture of sour cream.

3 Mix the shallot mixture and the Sriracha into the soft butter until evenly blended. Lay out a large sheet of plastic wrap, then spoon the butter onto it in a large mound in the center. Start to wrap the plastic up into a tube shape, using your hands to shape and smooth the butter. Pop it in the freezer for 2 hours, or leave it in the fridge overnight.

4 Light your grill on fire to the hottest it will go. Season the steaks liberally with salt and pepper—it should look like fresh snow just fell on that meat—then, when the grill is up to lightning temperature, throw them on.

Recipe Continues

5 Heat is good, but egregious flare-ups are bad, so keep those in check. Turn the steaks 90 degrees about 6 minutes in to get those super-dope cross-hatch marks, and then cook for another 5 minutes before flipping and repeating the same on the other side. I'd recommend using a meat thermometer, because humans suck at stuff, and try and get those bad boys to 145°F inside.

6 When the steaks are up to temp, throw them on a big-ass serving platter and put a whole bunch of that shallot Sriracha butter on top immediately so it can melt over everything. Let the steaks rest for 5 minutes (10 is totally overkill), then slice them up.

ANCHO- & ESPRESSO- RUBBED TRI-TIP

SERVES 6

1½ tablespoons salt

2 tablespoons finely ground espresso powder

2 tablespoons ancho chile powder

1 teaspoon black pepper

1 teaspoon ground cumin

1 teaspoon garlic powder

1 teaspoon onion powder

½ teaspoon cocoa powder

½ teaspoon ground cinnamon

2 tablespoons vegetable oil

1 (4-pound) tri-tip, fat preferably untrimmed (use a NY strip loin if you can't find tri-tip)

Motherfuckin' Bobby Flay, man. I think I've logged more hours staring at his face than any other face in the world. Which sounds sad now that I write it down, but one person's sad is another's totally fucking awesome. He was on all the time. *Iron Chef America, Boy Meets Grill, Grill It! with Bobby Flay, Beat Bobby Flay, Throwdown with Bobby Flay:* Bobby Flay became my cool digital uncle who would teach me all the useful things in life, like how to drink dark liquor in a backyard and how to cook giant primal cuts of meat over fire. And 99.999 percent of the time he was making some sort of ancho- and-espresso-rubbed something and a liquored-up sangria. Sometimes you just gotta ask yourself, "What would Bobby Flay do?" This.

---

1 Mix the salt, espresso powder, and all the spices together in a mixing bowl. Rub the oil all over the tri-tip, and then liberally sprinkle the spice blend all over the meat, rubbing it into the flesh with your hands. Wrap the meat in plastic wrap and let it sit in the fridge for a few hours (low-key though, that step is kind of unnecessary. The flavors will permeate the meat deeper, but also waiting sucks. So do whatever).

2 Heat only the outside burners of your grill, or, if you don't have one of those big-ass monster grills, just heat one side of it. Tri-tip is such a thick cut that you really have to cook it with indirect heat; otherwise, you're going to get scorched-but-raw beef. No one wants that.

3 If your grill has a temperature gauge, try and keep the heat pretty stable at around 500°F. Roast this thing real quick and dirty. Throw the tri-tip on a non-flame part of the grill, close the lid to get the heat up, then walk away.

4 Check on the meat every 5 minutes or so—just to make sure the grill isn't flaring up—and flip it periodically to cook evenly. After about half an hour, stick a meat thermometer in the thick part of it. You're looking for 140°F, which is pretty rare, but rare tri-tip is the shit. And since the end is thinner, the people who get weirded out by rare meat can all enjoy some medium-well bullshit.

5 When you see 140°F, torch the tri-tip in the hot part of the grill for 2 or 3 minutes, just to get some more color on there. Let it rest for 5 to 10 minutes, then slice as thinly as possible and sprinkle some salt on it. God, Bobby Flay would be proud.

MEXICAN CANDY SPARE RIBS

SERVES 6

2 racks pork spare ribs, fat trimmed and silverskin removed

3 tablespoons salt

2 teaspoons black pepper

1 (8-ounce) package tamarind paste

¼ cup apple cider vinegar

2 tablespoons honey

2 tablespoons soy sauce

1 minced chipotle in adobo

¼ cup Tajín Clásico seasoning (use 3 tablespoons chili powder if you can't find Tajin)

1 bunch scallions, thinly sliced (optional)

2 Fresno chilies, thinly sliced (optional)

When I was a kid, my dad worked at a 99-cent store. He had lost one career and needed something to pay the bills while he looked for another.

It wasn't a nice 99-cent store either. It wasn't one of those ironic ones that Orange County moms shopped at just to see what life was like for normal, non-SUV-driving people. This was your average strip-mall joint in a bad part of North San Diego County, and I would hang out there for hours on end. I'd skate in the alley out back—landed my first kickflip there—and occasionally my brother and I would set up a lemonade stand out front and use the profits to buy donuts from the shop across the street.

I was old enough to know that status was an important thing, and that I was supposed to be ashamed of my family not having enough of it. But I was also young enough that a 99-cent store was the raddest fucking place alive to be brought up in. The owner would rip the packaging off Frisbees and knockoff Nerf balls and let my brother and me play with them in the alley.

But the single best thing about the 99-cent store was its encyclopedic stash of Mexican candies and snack cakes. I ate all of them, all the time. Childhood obesity be damned. Gansito, Sponch, Duvalin, de la Rosa marzipan powder—the best things in life are $.99. There was one product that rearranged everything I knew about food: Pulparindo.

It's a mixture of tamarind paste, salt, citric acid, chili powder, sugar, and pure fucking magic. You squeeze it out of a tube straight into your mouth and it's equal parts sweet, spicy, and acidic and all those flavors are magnified and taken to their proper exponents. Candy that was so spicy it burned your throat and so sour it made your teeth itch. It was a total game changer in my life and essential to my food consciousness. I put all the flavors of Pulparindo into a pork-appropriate BBQ sauce. It's fucking good.

1 Preheat your oven to 300°F. Season up the ribs with the salt and pepper evenly divided between the two racks, then throw them on a baking sheet and toss them in the oven for 3 hours, until super tender.

2 In a medium saucepot on high heat, whisk together the tamarind paste, ½ cup water, vinegar, honey, soy sauce, and chipotle. Bring the mixture to a boil and reduce for 5 or 6 minutes, whisking constantly, until the mixture is thick and syrupy.

3 Cut the racks of ribs into two sets of four. Light your grill on high—as high as it will go. Burn those motherfuckers to the ground: Brush the ribs with some of your viscous tamarind mixture, then char the ribs on the grill until the sugars caramelize, about 3 minutes. Flip and repeat the same.

4 Put the ribs onto a baking sheet, then lacquer with more tamarind sauce. Take your Tajín and evenly dust it across the top of the ribs. Really get a bunch of it on there—Tajín is the tits.

5 Garnish with some thinly sliced scallions if you feel like you need some green shit on there, and some thinly sliced fresh Fresno chilies if you think you need some red shit.

MEXICAN CANDY
SPARE RIBS, *page 173*

PORK CHOPS
with
Burnt Applesauce

———

SERVES 4

4 large Gala apples (or something
    equivalent)

Vegetable oil

2 shallots

2 (12- to 16-ounce) bone-in
    Berkshire (or some equivalent
    breed) pork chops

Salt

Black pepper

2 tablespoons butter

2 tablespoons apple cider vinegar

1 teaspoon honey

1 teaspoon chopped fresh thyme

1 teaspoon fresh lemon juice

½ teaspoon cardamom

⅛ teaspoon ground nutmeg

Flaked salt

Pork chops are one of the few food items I'll be an asshole about when it comes to buying and sourcing. The normal commodity stuff from the grocery store is absolute inedible trash, especially when you compare it to some well-marbled chop from a heritage-breed pig. I learned this lesson as a hammered-drunk teen. You know, when most life lessons are learned.

My brother bought me a ticket to this heritage breed pig cookoff/ *Eyes Wide Shut*–style pork orgy called Cochon555 for my birthday (really, really consider going if they come to your city). There were a bunch of whiskey and wine purveyors, so I drank like it was the end of the world because I was bright-eyed and fresh-faced and things like this were still exciting back then. The amount of pork was dizzying. Ditto for the bourbon.

There was pork fat ice cream, raw Iberico pig sashimi, and a whole roast suckling pig on top of what the competing chefs made. Each of the different pig breeds had a unique taste and look and texture and marbling, and it was like being a kid in a candy store except dope-ass pork is better than candy. There was no going back to the grocery store shit after that.

This recipe is a pretty pure expression of pork—pig and applesauce is one of those classic combos—so I would implore you to actually go out of your way and at least get some chops from your local butcher. It really will make the difference.

1 You should go charcoal for this. The flavor of the charcoal is what's going to give your apples that smoky deliciousness. So light up that firebox and make it hot.

2 Peel the apples, slice them in half, core them, then cover them in a little bit of vegetable oil. Peel the shallots but leave them whole, coat in some vegetable oil, then throw all of that on the hottest part of the grill over the coals. Get some good char on both, about 10 minutes.

3 Once you get some color on them, make a tinfoil packet with at least three layers of foil and wrap the apples and shallots up real tight so no moisture escapes. Throw the whole thing directly onto the coals or right next to the coals. They're going to get some mad roasty flavor that way.

4 You're going to leave the apples and shallots there for about 15 minutes, flipping the packet halfway through, so you might as well start cooking your pork chops, yeah? Simply season them up with salt and pepper—real liberal-like—and rub them with vegetable oil, then throw on the hot part of the grill.

5 Sear for 4 minutes on one side, then turn 90 degrees to get those cartoonish cross-hatch grill marks that mean nothing; but, whatever, they look cool. Sear another 4 minutes, then flip and repeat the process. Use a meat thermometer and get that pork up to 150°F. You're looking for a perfect medium, with a little bit of that raw texture still there.

6 Pull off the pork chops and let them rest on a serving dish or something. The apples and shallots should now be super tender and taste like fire, so take them out of the package and throw them in the food processor, along with the butter, cider vinegar, honey, thyme, lemon juice, cardamom, nutmeg, ½ teaspoon salt, and ½ teaspoon pepper. Process continuously for at least 2 minutes, stopping halfway through to scrape down the sides.

7 Lay down a bed of your burnt applesauce, then slice the pork and arrange on top. Sprinkle with some flaked salt.

Burgers

THE

Tour De FIERI

5 BROS.

24 HOURS.

1,000 MILES.

3 RESTAURANTS.

▶ Guy Fieri was coming. Face dangerously close to purple, eyes beady but bulging, and hair violently spiked, he lumbered down a narrow corridor out of the back entrance of Tex Wasabi's where we—me, Marcus, Emil, Daesong, and Sander—were standing stupidly, all stupidly wearing matching Guy Fieri T-shirts that we'd stupidly bought an hour earlier at another one of his restaurants.

He started yelling: "Hey! Hey! Who the fuck is out here trying to take pictures of me?"

We froze in abject terror but every single part of me wanted him to punch one of us in the face because holy shit, could you imagine coming back with that story?

"Haha, I'm just kidding, guys. What's up? Heard you were all big fans," he said as he bro-hugged all of us one by one.

I always assume that people on TV are tiny, because most people on TV are tiny. And when you look at Guy Fieri on screen, he has the blocky, limbless dimensions of someone who would be tiny. He's massive.

He's only about six feet tall, but every single one of his features is twice the size it should be. His head, his hands, his two-toned goatee—every part of him dwarfs every part of you.

Guy asked us what we were doing, and what the deal was with the matching shirts, and why we spent 20 minutes arguing with a bouncer, and then another bouncer, and then a manager, and then his personal assistant to try and bait him out of his first-born son's birthday party.

So we told him about the trip. We told him about the Tour de Fieri.

How It All Started

The concept was simple: Three of us hop in a car, drive 500 miles up to Santa Rosa to meet up with the other two, eat and drink at three Guy Fieri–owned restaurants in one night, then drive 500 miles back within 24 hours. The reasons we were doing it were confusing, or, more accurately, completely nonexistent.

I wish I could say it was something cool, like we were all chasing Guy Fieri's legacy of cars and male bonding through a bro-y road trip, or that it was like *Julie & Julia* but with more dark liquor and we all figured out our lives through getting fucked up and eating tuna wonton tacos. But we were just bored. We were in college, it was summer, and we all had jobs that we only had to show up at twice a week.

More importantly, we already had a name for the trip. So we had to do it.

Sander and I ate egg foo yung that he stole off someone's doorstep on the drive up to Santa Barbara to pick up Emil, then we swung by Popeye's and continued up to Santa Rosa to meet up with Marcus and Daesong. The car smelled like fried chicken and gravy the whole trip, which seemed fitting.

We didn't roll into Santa Rosa until 5:30 p.m., and we didn't leave Marcus's apartment for another hour because we thought it was necessary to aggressively pregame. We had all just turned 21, which meant that it was necessary to aggressively pregame everything. Wedding? Pregame. Midterm? Pregame. Funeral? Bro...gotta pregame for that. It's what Gam-Gam would have wanted.

So we drank. We drank a lot. We drank whiskey and beer and gin and then hopped in a cab to the first stop.

The plan was to go to Johnny Garlic's in Windsor for appetizers, Johnny Garlic's in Santa Rosa for entrées, and then Tex Wasabi's—Guy Fieri's one-time pride and joy—for after-dinner drinks and dessert. Guy has since cut ties with every single restaurant we visited that night. At least we have our memories.

ROUND 1:
JOHNNY GARLIC'S,
WINDSOR

It's in a strip mall, but it's not the kind of endearing and self-aware strip mall restaurant that uses high-low irony to its benefit. It belongs in a strip mall. It's the "EZ Vape for You" of restaurants.

We got shots of Jack Daniels and shared a giant fish bowl filled with bright red liquor juice and maraschino cherries and oranges and sugar and little plastic fish toys. I can't speak to the quality of their entire cocktail program, but their fish bowls are cheap, non-offensive tasting, and highly drunkening. One million stars out of a possible one million. Nailed it.

There was no way we were leaving without the Ahi Won Tacos. Those are an OG Guy Fieri dish right there, and they were fantastic. Little bits of ice-cold raw tuna, mango salsa, and wasabi crema sitting in little fucking adorable fried wontons shaped like a Taco Bell taco.

It was the distilled essence of any whimsical and faux-trendy TGI Friday's appetizer, except no mass-market restaurant would risk serving raw fish for $9. That gaping hole in the industry is where Guy swooped in.

The garlic fries were great. Crispy on the outside but still tender and pulpy on the inside, then drowned in fresh raw garlic, butter, parsley, and Parmesan. Garlic fries are a California classic, Guy Fieri is a California motherfucker, and I was bloated with home-state pride and also dangerous levels of sodium and alcohol.

But, overall, there were more misses than hits. There was a noxious combo of cheese and hoisin sauce on a pork belly flatbread, AKA the epitome of Asian fusion gone horribly wrong. The lily-white, flaccid fried calamari made me want to apologize to every Italian person I've ever known. A cheesy seafood dip made me think of every episode of *Kitchen Nightmares* where Gordon Ramsay yelled, "These scallops are fucking rancid!" and threw a

plate at a 19-year-old line cook. Still, no one seemed to mind the objective shittiness.

We took more shots of Jack and we were all like, *Wooooooooo!* and we bought novelty Johnny Garlic T-shirts that had the same general aesthetic but varying degrees of severity in their motorcycle, hot-rod, and flame logos.

ROUND 2:
JOHNNY GARLIC'S,
SANTA ROSA

Like the Johnny Garlic's in Windsor, this Johnny Garlic's was in a strip mall, albeit a much nicer strip mall. It was one of those sterile corporate-park strip malls that would have a single Applebee's in it surrounded by nothing else, and it would constantly be filled with middle managers who under-tip.

As is customary during the Tour de Fieri, we started the meal off with shots of Jack and another punch bowl, except this one was filled with delicious electric blue sugar liquor. The last one was red. The blue one was better but only because it was blue. Both are still one million stars out of one million though—that rating hasn't changed.

We put in our dinner order. I don't think anyone gave a shit at this point what we were ordering, including me.

First out was the Cajun Chicken Alfredo. Guy Fieri claims he invented the dish while he was in culinary school. There's no way this can possibly be confirmed, but I love me a good origin myth.

There were five penne noodles in this bowl of fettuccine, which was confusing. Was someone in the back just negligently slapping at boxes of pasta until a sampling fell into the water? I couldn't even complain to anyone, because what was there to complain about? There are noodles in my noodles?

Then came the Maui Grilled Chicken Breast or something. It came with a nest of fried onions on top, which is a thing that I generally enjoy. The chicken itself was fine. The sauce was sickly sweet. The garlic mash tasted like mashed potatoes and the green beans tasted like green beans.

There was something else on the plate too: a big-ass pink flower. I asked my server if I was supposed to eat the flower. She said no. Then a manager came over and said that yeah, I could definitely eat

that flower and then lingered there like he wanted to watch me eat the flower. The server lingered to make sure I didn't eat the flower, so now I was forced to choose sides between the server and the manager, who seemed to have some long-standing tension with each other and the manager had more desperation in his eyes so I ate the flower and then my tummy hurt.

Fucking flower.

ROUND 3:
TEX WASABI'S,
SANTA ROSA

Last stop: Dessert Town, population us, bro, *Wooooo!* Sander called the restaurant from the cab to see what time they closed. There was disappointment in his voice as he hung up. Sander informed us that Tex Wasabi's was closed for the night due to a private event, and that the Tour de Fieri would have to be called off.

Then Marcus said something really cool. He goes, "It's gotta be him. It's gotta be Guy." And we were like, "Whaaaaaaat?" because it sounded like something someone in a movie would say. Apparently it's common Santa Rosa knowledge that Guy Fieri

will only rent out Tex Wasabi's to himself. We stayed the
course.

I walked up to a bouncer
parked at the back door, music
pouring from the building, and
said, "Oh, hey man, is there
something going on tonight?"

"Yes sir, the restaurant is
closed tonight for Mr. Fi-eddy's
son's birthday. He turned
eighteen today." It was weird
because he said it like he was
personally proud of Hunter
Fieri for making it to adulthood.

I told the bouncer about
the Tour de Fieri, and how we
drove 500 miles to get here
and we had already eaten at
two restaurants and we bought
matching T-shirts and for
fuck's sake can we just please
come in for a slice of cake?

That bouncer went and got
his boss, a bigger bouncer. We
explained the situation to him.
He walked away and brought a
third bouncer. Again, the story.
He left to get the general manager. At this point I had gotten
really good at telling our tale so
I knew where to add flourishes
and when to wait for gasps and
laughs. I was really glad I had
all those practice bouncers.

The general manager went
and got Guy's personal assistant. She came to vet us and
ask who or what we were and
why the fuck we were there,

which was a hard question even for us to answer. But apparently I answered correctly. She was going to go talk to Guy. We waited a full 15 minutes in the parking lot without seeing anyone else's face.

I had given up hope and was talking to Daesong about maybe leaving, or maybe jumping a fence and sneaking in through a side door. Dae's jaw dropped and he slowly lifted his finger to point directly behind me, the way a toddler in a horror movie would point at a ghost only she could see.

There he was, Guy Fieri, the Mayor of Flavortown himself, walking with his chest tastefully puffed, the way an overconfident, over-drunk dude-bro might walk up to a bartender to try and get her number.

He wasn't in full Guy Fieri costume. There were zero flames on his blue and white checkered button-down and the back of his head was completely devoid of sunglasses. He was moderately adorned with two studded chain bracelets, a small gold hoop in each ear, and a mobster-size ring on his right pinky. This was Guy Fieri the dad, not trying to take any attention away from his son's big day.

We talked about the Tour de Fieri, and about my eventual life goal of visiting every single restaurant he'd ever been to on *Diners, Drive-Ins and Dives* and interviewing the owners.

A few times he stopped us mid-sentence and burst out laughing at the fact that we were all wearing Johnny Garlic T-shirts, and then we'd start laughing because he was laughing.

Guy invited us into the party under the condition that none of us take any pictures or get too shitty off of free beer.

Tex Wasabi's is half sushi bar, half smokehouse, and three quarters bizarre two-story nightclub. It almost looks like a TGI Friday's concept store where the company was experimenting with an aggressive new rebrand strategy. I mean that all in a good way, in case there is any confusion.

Guy gave us the tour of the party. He pointed towards the biggest TV in the dining room where a montage of selfie-style videos played on loop. We couldn't hear what the people were saying, so Guy turned it up, just as Kid Rock was saying, "You're the man, Hunter!" He proudly explained that he got all his closest friends to record messages for his kid, including Matthew McConaughey and Raiders fullback Marcel Reece.

Say what you want about Guy Fieri, but that man fucking loves his family. I said a version of that to his face and he smiled and decided to suspend his no pictures policy so we could take a group shot.

Not wanting to overstay our welcome, we said our sweet goodbyes to Guy and gave him one last hug for the road. His assistant stopped us on the way out and told us to come back the next morning before the restaurant opened and to have brunch on the house.

ROUND 3.5: TEX WASABI'S,
SANTA ROSA

It was 10 a.m. and Tex Wasabi's was completely empty except for us five and the staff. Dishes just started hitting the table as soon as we sat down. Guy's buffalo sauce–drenched Vegas Fries with Bleu-Sabi, Killer Pork Egg Rolls with Eel Sauce, Potstickers, Pulled Pork Sliders, and the Jackass Roll, a soy paper–wrapped sushi roll with pulled pork, avocado, and orange mayonnaise.

The manager came over to talk to us. She said Guy told her about us, and how we were big fans of his, and how we traveled all this way just to eat at Tex

Wasabi's, and how grateful they both were for people like us.

She seemed incredibly genuine about everything. I deal with a lot of PR people and restaurant managers in situations like this for work, and you can tell who pretended to drink the Kool-Aid and who chugged it. This woman housed the whole damn pitcher.

Her eyes lit up when she explained the origin story of a dish. Guy was hosting a back-yard BBQ and sushi extrav-aganza for his buddies one day, she told us. He eventually ran out of ahi, and instead of letting all that sushi rice go to waste, he started packing rolls full of smoked pork shoulder. That's when his friend said to him, "You can't put pulled pork in sushi, you jackass." Thus, the Jackass Roll was born.

She pointed to the Vegas Fries and kept going. When Guy was in hospitality school at UNLV, he would frequent this one bar near campus that had killer Buffalo wings. He was so broke one night that he couldn't afford wings, so he asked the bartender to toss his fries in buffalo sauce.

She was so well-rehearsed that it would have been easy to call bullshit, but at the same time I could imagine either of those scenarios happening to

me. You could probably find five stories just like those ones in the headnotes of this book.

Everything we had at Tex Wasabi's was solid. It was basically the best version of Applebee's-style food that could possibly exist, which is exactly what it intends to be. I was riding high snorting lines of Guy Fieri Kool-Aid powder, but I still couldn't reconcile how relatively shit our meals at the two Johnny Garlic's were.

How could anyone I respect put their name on such a mediocre institution, and

do nothing to change it? Then I asked myself the question: What would I really do if I were in Guy Fieri's shoes?

If I could slap my name on a building, do absolutely nothing, and collect a check, I would do it in a heartbeat, and you probably would too. Even Anthony Bourdain, who con-stantly shits on Guy Fieri and other food world sellouts, sold out to host a cooking game-show on ABC.

Get me a fishbowl full of Kool-Aid and Everclear and rim the glass with Donkey Sauce.

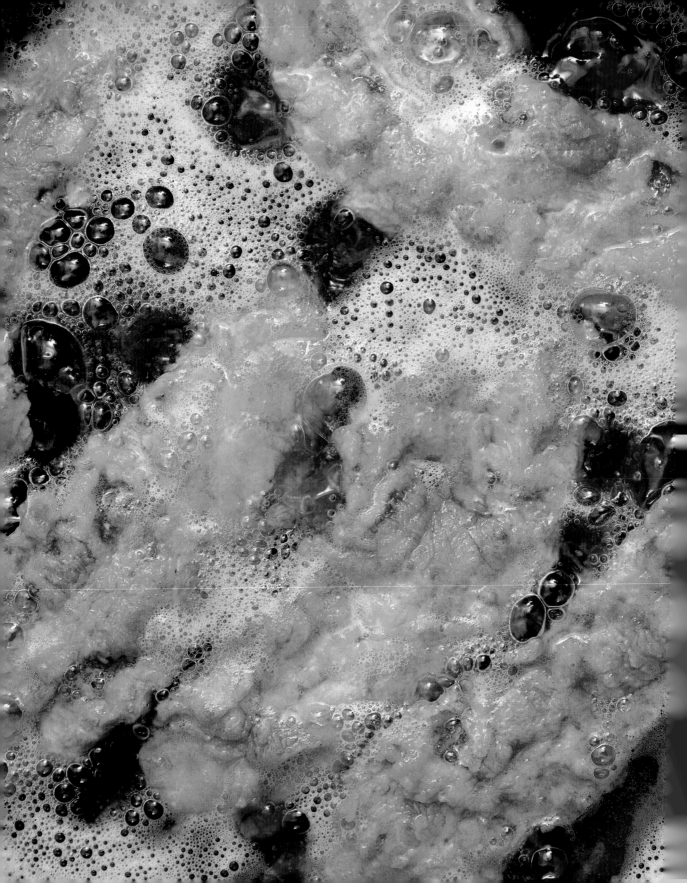

CHICKEN-FRIED-BACON BURGERS

MAKES 4 BURGERS

8 strips bacon

2 cups plus 1 tablespoon flour

Salt

2¼ cups whole milk

6 eggs

Vegetable oil, for frying

1 tablespoon unsalted butter

Black pepper

1½ pounds 80/20 ground beef

4 slices sharp cheddar cheese

4 English muffins

This is to prove my theory that chicken-frying all your meats makes them infinitely better. I mean, just think about fried chicken for a second. Chicken isn't that great of a meat, but fried chicken might be the best dish of all time. So the secret has to be in the process, right? And chicken-fried steak only reifies the theory. We—and by *we* I mean society eternal—took perfectly good steak, smashed the fuck out of it until it was paper thin, dredged it in crunchies, popped it in a fryer, and turned it into the single best hangover-curing meat disc that's ever existed. Why shouldn't the same rule of science apply to bacon? It should. It does.

1 Cut each slice of bacon in half, because that hanging-comically-far-off-the-bun shit doesn't fly here. Dump 2 cups of the flour into a large mixing bowl and stir in 1 teaspoon salt. In a separate mixing bowl, whisk together the ¼ cup milk and 2 of the eggs. Coat your bacon strips in flour, then in egg wash, then back into the flour. Really mash the flour into the bacon on the second pass to make sure it's all coated.

2 Fill a large sauté pan—the biggest one you have—with 1 inch of vegetable oil. Heat on high until the oil starts to shimmer and move freely. Place the bacon strips in, working in batches to not overcrowd the pan. Flip after about 3 minutes and continue to cook on the other side until golden brown, about 2 minutes. Remove from the pan and let them drain on a paper towel. Or don't use a paper towel—excess grease is only going to improve the burger.

3 Heat a small nonstick saucepot on medium and add the butter. When the butter is melted, stir in the 1 tablespoon flour. Continue to stir with a wooden spoon until the mixture becomes a light amber color. Add the remaining 2 cups milk, ½ teaspoon salt, and ¼ teaspoon pepper; stir until there are no lumps left. Turn the heat off and save the gravy for later.

4 Form the ground beef into ¼-pound patties about the diameter of your English muffin and season both sides liberally with salt and pepper. Heat a large sauté pan—or cast-iron skillet if you have one—on high heat with 1 tablespoon vegetable oil. When the oil starts to smoke, sear your patties for about 3 minutes, then flip, add cheese, and cook another 3 minutes. You want a heavy crust to form, but you also want some pink in the middle.

5 Fry the remaining 4 eggs sunny-side up. If you don't know how to do that... I don't know, man; fucking google it and improve your life.

6 Toast the English muffins, then top each with a burger patty, chicken-fried bacon strips, gravy, and a fried egg. Congratulations, you just ate 2,000 calories for breakfast!

LAMB PATTY
MELTS
with
Fennel Jam

MAKES 4 BURGERS

Fennel Pomegranate Jam

6 medium fennel bulbs

2 tablespoons butter

1 cup brown ale

¼ cup pomegranate molasses

Harissa Thousand Island

¼ cup mayonnaise

2 tablespoons ketchup

1 tablespoon harissa paste (comes in a tube; is dope)

½ teaspoon Worcestershire sauce

½ teaspoon lemon juice

2 tablespoons finely minced green olives

6 to 8 fresh mint leaves, finely minced

Burgers

1 tablespoon salt

1 teaspoon cumin

1 teaspoon smoked paprika

½ teaspoon coriander

½ teaspoon black pepper

1 pound ground lamb

2 tablespoons oil

8 ounces Gruyère, shredded

8 slices seeded rye bread

2 tablespoons butter

I am Jewish. I know this because I once got a free two-week vacation to Israel for being Jewish. I wish I could say I fell in love with the flavors of the homeland, but I didn't. Don't get me wrong, I ate some pretty dope hummus and found out that cold eggplant and hard-boiled eggs in pita makes for way better drunk food than I thought. But za'atar kind of sucks and eating cucumbers for breakfast is a custom I'm deeply uncomfortable with. The trip did make me more Jewish though. Just a little. It inspired me to fuck around in the old-school, Jewish-owned delis and diners in L.A.—the kind where you can get a patty melt and chopped liver on toast at 3 a.m. Smashing some greasy lamb in rye bread is about as culturally sentimental as I can get.

1 **For the jam:** Trim each fennel bulb by cutting off all the stalks and slicing about ½ inch off the tough butthole end of it. If you have a mandoline, use that to slice it as thinly as humanly possible. If you don't, just cut each bulb in half down the prime meridian, flip it so the flattest side is on the cutting board, then go to town with a knife.

2 Heat the butter on medium-high heat in a large skillet, and when it's melted, throw in all your fennel. You're going to have to stir this shit for a while until the fennel actually starts to break down and caramelize, which sucks, and I sympathize with you, but it's totally worth it.

3 After about 20 minutes, when the fennel is broken down and starting to caramelize, crank the heat to high, and get a little extra char on it. Add 1 cup of water, the ale, and the pomegranate molasses. Keep stirring as the mixture boils down and eventually looks like jam, about 10 minutes. Set the jam aside to cool.

4 **For the thousand island:** Just stir it all together in a bowl.

5 **To assemble the burgers:** In a small bowl, stir together the salt and all the spices and set aside.

6 Divide the lamb into 4 equal lumps. Heat the oil on high heat in a heavy-bottomed sauté pan or a cast-iron skillet. When the oil starts to smoke, lay down the lumps of lamb meat. Leave them in lump form, and let them sear just like that for 30 seconds. Then, with a spatula, start smashing them into the pan. Don't worry about shape or symmetry—there is only smash now.

7 When the burgers are sufficiently smashed and charred, sprinkle liberally with your spice mixture on one side, then flip, give them another quick smash with the spatula, hit them with some more magic spice dust, then throw your shredded cheese on top and let it melt.

8 Take a slice of rye bread and top with a schmear of harissa thousand island, then the smashed lamb burger, then a heaping helping of fennel jam, then more thousand island, then top with more bread. Heat that butter in a large sauté pan on high, then toast each side of the burgers, grilled-cheese style, until golden brown.

THE FAT HAWAIIAN BURGER

MAKES 4 BURGERS

1 (12-ounce) can SPAM

2 tablespoons plus 1 quart vegetable oil

¼ cup bottled teriyaki sauce

3½ cups flour

1 egg

1½ cups ice-cold soda water

1 shot vodka

4 pineapple rings (from a 20-ounce can)

1 pound ground pork

Salt

Black pepper

4 slices white American cheese (get Swiss-style American if you can)

4 King's Hawaiian hamburger buns (or use any white bun if you can't find them)

1 bunch scallions

3 tablespoons mayonnaise

1 tablespoon Sriracha

The first time I had pineapple on pizza it was the fanciest thing I'd ever eaten. Maybe fancy isn't the right word, but it was definitely gourmet. Or maybe epicurean. Yeah, I like that word. Epicurean shit like pineapples and olives and anchovies—that's what adults eat. Only kids fuck with pepperoni. The same concept translated over to burgers. Anytime I see one of those pineapple and teriyaki deals on a menu, that instinct kicks in and I impulsively order it. Then I impulsively eat it. Then I go home and impulsively make it, except I do it on my terms—with a fuckton of SPAM and deep-fried fruit.

1 Slice SPAM into eight ¼-inch-thick sheets. Slice lengthwise so they're more cylindrical than square. Heat 1 tablespoon of the oil in your largest sauté pan on high heat until it shimmers and moves freely, then sear off your canned ham slices, making sure to really crisp them up good. You know what, fuck it, straight up burn them. SPAM is at its best when it's super-carcinogenic. Flip them and repeat the searing process. When both sides are nice and charred, throw in the teriyaki sauce and turn off the heat, moving the meat slabs around the pan to evenly coat with sauce, which should be thick and caramelized. Set them on a plate and reserve for later.

2 Heat the 1 quart oil on high heat in a large Dutch oven, or a deep saucepan, or a deep fryer, but you probably don't have a deep fryer, because deep fryers are annoying as shit. The target temp is 375°F.

3 Set out two large mixing bowls. In the first, throw in 2 cups of the flour. In the second, combine the egg with the remaining 1½ cups flour, the cold soda water, and 1 shot of vodka. (Pour a shot of vodka for yourself. You've earned it, champ.) Whisk that tempura batter real good. Like, real good. Put some fucking effort in.

4 Crack open that delicious can of pineapple and drain 4 rings really well. Lay out a bunch of paper towels and pat each ring dry. Dredge those bad boys in flour—really mash the flour in there—then coat them fully in the tempura batter. Carefully drop the pineapple rings in your 375-degree oil. You want them to crisp up as fast as possible, because there's so much moisture in pineapple that it can explode on you real quick. Gotta move fast. After 30 seconds. Flip each ring, then fry for an additional 30 seconds, until golden brown. Remove with tongs or a fork or something and let them drain on paper towels. Reserve for later.

5 Form your ground pork into four ¼-pound patties roughly the diameter of your bun. (AKA: Just make it into a fucking burger. You've been here before.) Season liberally with salt and pepper. Heat a tablespoon of vegetable oil in a heavy-bottomed sauté pan until it's screaming hot. Throw in those patties and sear for roughly 2 minutes on one side, or until nice and charred. Then flip, add the cheese, and continue to cook for another 2 minutes, or, you know, until cooked through in the middle so you won't die of trichinosis or whatever.

6 Toast those buns up in a pan. Slice the whole bunch of scallions as thin as humanly possible. Whisk together the mayo and Sriracha, then lather up both sides of a bun with that delicious, universal condiment. Throw a generous handful of scallions on the bottom bun, top it with a burger patty, then some teriyaki SPAM, then a tempura pineapple ring, then bun that shit up.

THE FAT HAWAIIAN BURGER, *page 192*

CHILI-CHEESE JUCY LUCYS

MAKES 4 BURGERS

Nonstick cooking spray

1 (15-ounce) can of your favorite chili (let's bring canned chili back)

2 pounds 80/20 ground beef

8 ounces Velveeta cheese

1 tablespoon oil

Salt

4 Kaiser rolls (try to find telera rolls if you can though)

Mayo (Seriously, just put mayonnaise on everything. Because it fucking deserves to be on everything.)

1 red onion, thinly sliced

1 jar pickled jalapeño rings

1 bunch fresh cilantro

1 small bag corn chips

WATCH OUT

THIS IS AN **OVERNIGHT** RECIPE

"But Josh, I don't have time or patience or foresight to make an overnight recipe," you might say, quite stupidly. Look, I take this shit seriously, OK? This is my art, and my art involves time, blood, sweat, tears, and dumping dented cans of chili that I got from the discount rack into the freezer and then gently inserting them into rounds of meat. And if that's a problem for you, then you can fuck right off. Or you can just make an easy tweak to the recipe and make the burger with just cheese inside, then microwave the chili and dump it on top. Or fuck off. That option is still very much on the table. Your choice.

For those of you who don't know, the Jucy Lucy—perfectly misspelled—is a burger with a bunch of cheese stuffed in the middle of the raw patty. When it's cooked, the cheese turns into a molten mass of yellow that's going to shoot down your throat and straight up burn your esophagus around, oh, let's say bite three. It's a magical experience. You know what makes it more magical? When you cheat god and freeze chili into a disc, stuff that inside the burger, and get a double helping of beefiness straight to the dome.

---

1 Line a baking sheet with parchment paper, then spray that shit down with nonstick cooking spray. Open your can of chili and place four 2-tablespoon dollops on the parchment paper. Spread them out until you have an even circular mound that is about 3 inches in diameter. Pop them in the freezer overnight. You want frozen chili discs. I hope you see where this is going. It's going to a really fantastic, borderline offensively stupid place. Let's do this.

2 The next day, form your ground beef into eight ¼-pound patties. You want them to be pretty thin and at least 4 inches in diameter. There's a lot of math here. Keep up.

3 Place a frozen disc of chili and an approximately equal amount of cheese on top of 4 of the burger patties. Use the remaining 4 burger patties as lids, placing them on the topped burgers, and making sure to seal around the edges. Try to form each into an even, puck-like shape while never letting the chili or cheese break through the burger's surface.

4 Heat the oil in a heavy-bottomed sauté pan on medium-high heat until it moves freely (you've been here before). Season the burgers with salt, then sear for 5 minutes on each side. You're gonna need to cook this longer than most burgers to ensure that the frozen chili disc thaws. Don't be afraid to poke your finger in there to make sure the chili's warm.

5 Toast up them Kaiser/telera rolls. Spread some mayo on a bottom bun, then throw down your monster burger patty. Top it with some red onion slices, pickled jalapeño rings, cilantro, and a liberal handful of corn chips. Add more mayo on the top bun, then smash that shit down.

THE
GAS STATION
BURGER

MAKES 4 BURGERS

1 (20-ounce) bottle cherry cola

¼ cup ketchup

2 chipotles in adobo, minced

¼ teaspoon smoked paprika

¼ teaspoon cumin

¼ teaspoon onion powder

½ teaspoon salt

½ teaspoon black pepper

8 strips thick-cut bacon

1 pound 80/20 ground beef

4 slices sharp cheddar

4 brioche buns

1 bag Flamin' Hot Funyuns

You guys fuck with that show *Chopped*? Man, I hope you're reading this while that show's still around because it's the single best thing Food Network's done since Sandra Lee's Kwanzaa cake. (YouTube it right now. The clip is only 2:45; this recipe can wait.) Four completely unknown contestants, all jacked up on promise and producers telling them to be all jacked up, run into a studio kitchen and they all get a basket filled with four random ingredients—razor clams, spicy red cheese sticks (legally they can't say Flamin' Hot Cheetos), fermented yak penis, and baby kale, for instance—and they all do a cooking battle against each other and there's an ominous clock and then they get more baskets and then the judges just fucking mercilessly shred them for undercooking their yak penis but then they find out one of the contestants' mom died or something and then the sympathetic music plays and the judges are all like, "Awwwww."

But the single best part is that when one episode ends and a champion is crowned, the next episode starts without you ever noticing. So you can just pass a whole day watching these strangers cook shit from a mystery box and then, without you noticing it, you end up alone in a gas station creating your own mystery box because TV and reality have become inseparable and you walk out with Flamin' Hot Funyuns and cherry cola and I HAVE TO MAKE A BURGER AND MAINLINE FOOD NETWORK RIGHT THE FUCK NOW.

1 Start out by making some sweet, sweet, diabetic cherry cola BBQ sauce. Empty those 20 ounces of soda into a medium saucepot and throw it on high heat. You want the soda to come to a boil and reduce down by about three quarters. It should take about 12 minutes. Then add the ketchup, minced chipotles, paprika, cumin, onion powder, salt, and pepper. Stir, drop to medium, and continue to reduce for another 2 minutes, or until it looks like BBQ sauce.

2 Heat a large sauté pan on medium-high heat. Place the bacon strips in the pan. Fry them in their own fat until they're looking all nice and crispy-like. Drain on paper towels.

3 Form the ground beef into ¼-pound patties and season liberally with salt. Ideally, you'd grill these over charcoal, but feel free to just throw them in a pan. It doesn't really matter. Nothing really matters. We all die in the end. But first, burgers! Sear the burger patties over as high a heat as you can figure out how to make, then melt a slice of cheddar over each one.

4 Toast them buns. Schmear some cherry cola BBQ sauce on the bottom bun, throw on a burger, then some bacon, then a hefty layer of those onion ring proxies. Then—and this is imperative—absolutely drown that shit in more cherry cola BBQ sauce. Smash the burger down with your fist so it fits in your mouth. Eat with beer. And then eat again with more beer.

DOUBLE
VEGGIE
BURGERS

MAKES 4 BURGERS

2 medium red beets

Salt

Olive oil

8 ounces cremini mushrooms

Black pepper

1 tablespoon soy sauce

1 tablespoon Worcestershire sauce

1 (12-ounce) block extra-firm tofu

4 ounces Soyrizo

½ cup roasted almonds

½ cup canned black-eyed peas

1 teaspoon smoked paprika

Dry breadcrumbs, if needed

8 ounces Gruyère cheese, shredded

4 whatever-the-fuck-burger-buns-you-want

¼ cup mayo

4 large butter lettuce leaves

4 slices hothouse tomato

Pickle slices to your liking

I want to pretend like I give a shit what happens to the planet after I die, and sometimes I even convince myself that I do give a shit, but, really, I don't. I've tried giving a shit, I really have. But every time I do, I end up not. I've gone vegan for a month at a time, and I just end up breaking that with a fucking chupacabra-style meat binge. Goat blood and all that.

I've tried buying ethically sourced meat from local farms, but the grocery store is cheaper and more convenient. People don't change. Statistically speaking, you don't give a shit either. You the individual might, but the universal you definitely doesn't.

So, why sub in a bunch of mashed-up vegetables and soy and shit for red meat? Because vegetables taste good. Like, on a chemical level. They were literally designed for you to put in your mouth and turn into usable energy, and now you can game the system even further by turning that into some decadent two-tier calorie tower.

---

1 Preheat your oven to 400°F and roast yourself some beets: Trim the stems and the ends off the beets, give them a rinse, then put each one in a foil packet with a pinch of salt and a drizzle of olive oil. Seal the packet and throw in the oven for about 45 minutes, until they're fork tender. Take them out, let them cool, then pulse in a food processor until they're all crumbly and stuff.

2 Cut the mushrooms into quarters, then throw them in the food processor (take the beets out first) and pulse until they're finely minced. Heat a cast-iron skillet, or a normal sauté pan, with 1 teaspoon olive oil until searing hot, and throw in the mushrooms. Add a liberal amount of salt and pepper along with the soy sauce and Worcestershire, then sauté for about 10 minutes, until the mixture is completely dry.

3 Now, get down with the tofu: Heat a large sauté pan over medium-high heat. Cut the block of the tofu in half through the equator, season liberally with salt, then throw the two halves in the hot pan. Put a pan on top of the tofu to compress it down and develop a nice crust. Really burn the fuck out of it. Flip and repeat on the other side.

4 Throw the beets, mushrooms, Soyrizo, and tofu into the food processor, along with the almonds, black-eyed peas, paprika, 1 teaspoon salt, and 1 teaspoon pepper. Let it run until you have a smooth-lookin' puree. If it looks too wet to form into patties, stir in some breadcrumbs. Shouldn't be too dry though.

5 Form the mush into eight relatively thin burger-sized patties—this is a double-up, after all. Sear in a hot pan with a liberal amount of olive oil. There's nothing you really have to cook, but the crispy burnt edges on the veggie patty means flavor development, so go big on the char.

6 Flip each patty and throw on a handful of shredded Gruyère until it melts. Throw one patty on top of another, then toss onto a mayo-slathered bun with lettuce, tomato, and pickles.

THE LAND, SEA & AIR BURGER

MAKES 2 BURGERS

6 tablespoons mayonnaise

1 tablespoon pickle relish

1 teaspoon lemon juice

8 ounces boneless skinless chicken breast (about half a large breast)

Salt

1 (8-ounce) whitefish fillet (cod, tilapia, or pollock work)

3 cups flour

¼ cup milk

2 eggs

12 ounces beer

Vegetable oil, for frying

4 slices American cheese

½ pound 80/20 ground beef

Black pepper

4 sesame seed buns (or whatever white bun, really)

1 tablespoon yellow mustard

2 tablespoons ketchup

Bunch of pickle slices

½ cup finely diced white onion

1 cup shredded iceberg lettuce

You know that "Ceci n'est pas une pipe" thing? Where it's a picture of a pipe, but the artist is all like, "This isn't a pipe, it's just a picture of a pipe, you limp-dicked fuck-up sorry-ass excuse for a person; how could you not figure that out without me scribbling it down?" Yeah, you know the one. Well, "Ceci n'est pas une burger," or whatever. You don't make the fabled Land, Sea & Air Burger to put it in your mouth and turn it into usable energy; you make it because you can. Fish from sea, cow from land, chicken from air—this shit is art. Or science. Or both. Or it's actually just the result of a time when I got drunk and went to McDonald's and threw a Filet-O-Fish patty and a McChicken cutlet into a cheeseburger. But that doesn't make it any less important.

1 Whisk 3 tablespoons of the mayonnaise with the pickle relish and lemon juice. This is makeshift tartar sauce. Reserve for later. Slice your chicken breast in half through the equator, then in half through the prime meridian (geography as fuck!). Then take 2 pieces of that chicken and wrap each loosely in plastic wrap. Use a blunt object—meat mallet, fist, never-opened textbook, whatever—to gently beat the shit out of them until they are about ½ inch thick. Unwrap each chicken sheet and season with salt.

2 Take the fish fillet and slice it so that you have 2 pieces that are of equal size and thickness as the chicken breast pieces. All should be about the same size as the buns you're using.

3 Dump 2 cups of the flour into a large mixing bowl and stir in 1 teaspoon salt and whatever other seasonings you feel like getting rid of. Throw the whole fucking spice rack in there—it really doesn't matter. In a separate mixing bowl, whisk together the milk and eggs. Coat your chicken breast sheets in flour, then in egg wash, then back into the flour. Really mash the flour into the chicken on the second pass to get that extra crispiness.

4 In yet another mixing bowl (art is complicated), whisk together the remaining 1 cup flour with the beer. Dredge the 2 fish fillets in the same flour mixture that you dredged the chicken in, then coat it in the beer batter.

5 Fill a large sauté pan with 2 inches of vegetable oil. Heat on medium-high until the oil starts to shimmer and move freely. Place the battered fish fillets in and fry for about 3 minutes on one side, then flip and cook for an additional 2 minutes, until golden brown. Remove the fish fillets, place a slice of American cheese on top of each, and let drain on a paper towel. The residual fish heat should melt the cheese.

Recipe Continues

6 Keep the pan on medium-high heat, and place the flour-crusted chicken sheets in and fry for about 3 minutes on each side, or until golden brown, crunchtastic, and cooked through. Remove and let drain on a paper towel.

7 Form your ground beef into two ¼-pound patties about the size of your buns and season both sides liberally with salt and pepper. Heat a sauté pan—or cast-iron skillet if you got one—on high heat with 1 tablespoon vegetable oil. When the oil starts to smoke, sear your patties for about 3 minutes, then flip, add one slice of cheese on top of each patty, and cook another 3 minutes. You want a heavy crust to form, but you also want some pink in the middle.

8 Cooking is the easy part. It's the architecture that's going to fuck you up. Just follow the layering process exactly like this and you shouldn't have a problem. OK? OK. Let's do it. For each of your two burgers, you go: bottom bun, burger patty with cheese, mustard, ketchup, pickles, onions; top bun, mayonnaise (remember that mayo you have left?), chicken, lettuce; bottom bun, fish fillet with cheese, tartar sauce; top bun. Boom. Art.

As much as I like using burgers as a canvas to fuck around on—and I really do—sometimes I just want to eat a really delicious and burger-y burger. But even then, what is burgeriness? Does it follow the In-N-Out model? Shake Shack? An old-school steakhouse? There's a place in L.A. right now called Everson Royce Bar that's doing the most burger-y burger I've ever had. It's incredibly simple too: Tillamook cheddar, Dijonnaise, and a griddle-cooked ¼-pound patty on a super-hard-toasted brioche bun. It's one of those burgers where the whole is like a million times greater than the sum of its parts. E.R.B. is my muse for this burger. Except I'm adding roasted garlic and roasted tomatoes and shallots because I really like all of those things.

THE
BURGER

—

MAKES 4 BURGERS

1 head garlic

Salt

Vegetable oil, for slickening things

4 large Roma tomatoes

2 small shallots

¼ cup red wine vinegar

½ teaspoon coarse sea salt

½ cup mayonnaise

2 tablespoons horseradish mustard (a strong Dijon is fine)

1 teaspoon lemon juice

½ teaspoon Worcestershire

½ teaspoon coarse ground black pepper

1 pound 70/30 ground beef

4 slices sharp white cheddar

4 brioche buns

1 Heat your oven to 400°F. Cut the top ¼ inch off the head of garlic and place it on a foot-long sheet of aluminum foil. Sprinkle with salt, drizzle with 2 teaspoons vegetable oil, and seal the foil tightly. Throw in the oven and let it roast for about 40 minutes, until the garlic has slightly browned. Throw it immediately in the freezer so it'll get cool enough to work with.

2 Core the tomatoes, slice them in half lengthwise, then toss them into a large mixing bowl. Drizzle with vegetable oil and sprinkle about a tablespoon of salt on them. Toss with your hands and space evenly apart on a baking sheet so they aren't touching. No touching! Leave room for Jesus as well as other gods in the name of inclusivity. Put the baking sheet in the oven, but watch out for the garlic. Don't forget it's in there. Roast the tomatoes for 25 to 30 minutes. You don't want them to get completely dried out, but you definitely want to see some char on them. Then let your tomatoes rest somewhere. Anywhere, really.

3 While the vegetables are roasting, peel the shallots and slice them as thinly as possible. Dump the vinegar into a tiny little bowl and then let your shallots soak in there until you're ready to apply them to the burger.

4 When the garlic is no longer molten hot, squeeze the asshole end of it until 8 cloves pop out. Mash up those cloves. Arrange them into a mound and hit them with the coarse sea salt. Use the flat edge of your knife to scrape the garlic against the cutting board. See what that's doing there? Creating a nice little paste? Yeah, you see it.

5 Whisk together your garlic paste with the mayo, mustard, lemon juice, Worcestershire, and black pepper. Let that hang out somewhere.

6 Form the ground beef into four ¼-pound patties and season each side liberally with salt. Heat 1 tablespoon vegetable oil on hot hot heat in a heavy-bottomed pan. Cast iron would be cool. When the oil starts to smoke, drop the burger patties in there. Let them sear off for about 3 minutes on one side, then flip, add your cheese, and sear for an additional 2 minutes.

7 Figure out a way to toast your buns. Any way is fine. I trust you. Slather both sides of your buns with that delicious roasted garlic mayo, then throw a cheese-y burger patty on top of that, then two pieces of that roasted tomato, then a few scattered bits of your vinegar marinated shallots.

8 Place the top bun on there, then promptly flip the burger upside down and let it rest on the top bun for at least 1 minute before eating. This will all make sense in time.

10

Fried Things

My older brother, Jon, and I are pretty much the same person. We have the same hobbies, thought processes, and—most importantly—taste in food. Sharing a pizza is real easy for us. We grew up cooking together and binge-watching Food Network together, and we still try to get together and fuck around in the kitchen as often as possible. Not long ago, I learned a dark secret about him: He's never deep-fried anything.

After he admitted this to me, quite ashamedly, I ran through the memory bank to see if I could picture him dipping corn dogs into oil, or straining out a funnel cake onto a bed of paper towels. Nothing. It was weird. Like half the time I'm making something serious in the kitchen, there's a deep-fried element somewhere in the equation. How could this happen?

I asked him why. He told me something I wasn't prepared to hear. He was...afraid. This is my older brother, whom I've looked up to my entire life, the one who threatened to beat up the kids who bullied me (that's not true, I've been bigger than him since I was eight years old, but go along with it for the story), and he was admitting fear over the process of making mac 'n' cheese fritters. It was a level of emotional vulnerability that I wasn't used to, and it freaked me out.

I told people about it, and they were more sympathetic with him than me. I learned that people I was close to—people I thought I knew—had also never deep-fried anything, solely out of fear. Not one chimichanga. Not one chicken wing. Not even a single jalapeño popper.

My entire worldview was shaken. Frying is a process that I've taken for granted for so long that I never even considered the possibility of living without it. So many of the best, most objectively delicious foods are deep-fried, and all these people have been deprived of making them in the comfort of their own home. It's a fucking travesty.

But I get it, you know. Pouring hot oil on people was like a medieval anti-siege warfare tactic or something, so there's definitely a precedent for it doing damage. And, more contemporarily speaking, turkey-frying accidents cause millions of dollars in property damage every year. That said, as long as you're a human being with a pretty-close-to-fully-functioning brain, you can easily deep-fry things without dying. And also prevent Visigoth hordes from storming your gates. Here are a few things to know.

You Don't Need an Actual Deep-Fryer

Deep-fryers are the fucking worst. At least the janky-ass, electric, countertop ones that they sell at Bed Bath & Beyond—or wherever—are the worst. It takes forever to heat up, the temperature gauge never actually works, it's the worst to clean, and it's just going to end up sitting on your porch collecting rain water after your first batch of mozzarella sticks melts into the oil and you're too lazy to deal with it. I know some people who live and die by the fryer, and I totally respect them, I just don't personally fuck with one.

Cast Iron Is Your Friend

My go-to frying appliance is a cast iron Dutch oven. It's deep but it also has a ton of surface area, and the cast iron is totally an ideal material because it's going to heat your oil more gradually and evenly than something like aluminum. That's only for when I'm doing a big fry job though. If I'm just frying up some herbs for a garnish, I'll heat a tiny amount of oil in a normal saucepot and drop the leaves in when the oil shimmers and moves freely across the pan.

Only Use Light Oils

Canola, vegetable, and peanut are the big three I like to use, with peanut taking the number one spot. Don't use olive oil, which is a dark oil. Olive oil is the most overrated ingredient in your pantry, and you should stop using it for most things. It has a low smoke point, which causes it to get bitter and it's just a bad situation all around.

Thermometers Are Encouraged for Beginners

If you're already afraid of deep-frying things, a thermometer will help ease that fear. The main bad thing that can happen while you're frying is that the oil spontaneously combusts and lights you on fire and you die. It's reasonable to be scared of that. But that only happens when the oil reaches a stupidly high temperature (generally past 700°F), which is only possible if you straight up fall asleep and forgot you were about to make some dope-ass Buffalo wings. At around 450°F, most light oils start to smoke, and if the oil starts to smoke, you know you've gone too far. In the unlikely event that the pot does catch fire, just clamp a lid down on it to suffocate the flames. Most things you'll be frying fall in the range of 350 to 375°F. I generally test the oil to see if it's hot enough by dropping in a pinch of flour. If it aggressively sizzles, it's good to go. But that method takes a good amount of time and practice and feel to master. You can't teach instinct. In the meantime, it's probably a good idea to invest in a thermometer.

Invest in a Legit Strainer

There's a specific type of strainer called a spider—wooden handle, wide wire basket—that you should definitely invest in. You can buy a cheap one online for less than $5, and it's the best less-than-$5 you'll ever spend, except for maybe a Taco Bell combo meal. Anyways, use a spider to remove your crispy deliciousness from the oil and let the excess oil drain on a bed of paper towels. If you don't have a strainer, you can totally use a slotted wooden spoon. Just make sure you don't use any all-metal tools, because they will transmit heat, and they will burn the fuck out of your hand. Oh and never use plastic tools in hot oil. I mean, unless you're really trying to get a protective melted plastic coating on your onion rings. If so, carry on.

Overcoming fears is a part of life. Chimichangas are also a part of life. Now you can kill two birds with one golden-brown, delicious stone.

JAGER BOMB FRITTERS,
page 213

JAGER BOMB
FRITTERS

MAKES 16 TO 20
FRITTERS

Sizzurp

1 (24-ounce) can non-diet energy
  drink

1 cup Jagermeister

Fritters

1 cup milk

1 egg

½ cup non-diet energy drink

¼ cup Jagermeister

2 cups flour

½ cup cornmeal

3 tablespoons sugar

1 teaspoon baking soda

1 teaspoon salt

Canola, vegetable, or peanut oil,
  for frying

Powdered sugar, for dusting

The first iteration of this recipe was meant to follow the same logic as vodka melon and rum ham: You take something delicious and soak it in liquor so you can eat tasty food and get drunk at the same time. Somehow I forgot that both vodka melon and rum ham are basically inedible, and anyone who has ever made either of those things more than once shouldn't be allowed to operate a motor vehicle. I made some Red Bull–heavy fritters, soaked them in straight Jager, dusted them with powdered sugar, and popped one in my mouth. The alcohol fumes made me cough and so I inhaled a fine dusting of powdered sugar deep into my lungs and then I threw up in the sink. The fact that it ended with me throwing up is pretty consistent with the Jager brand. The revised recipe, although not as alcoholic, is actually edible, bordering on tasty. And it totally has that nostalgic Jager Bomb flavor, which, for me, is associated with falling off a roof freshman year of college.

1 **For the sizzurp:** Heat a medium saucepan on high heat and add the energy drink and Jagermeister. Bring the mixture to a boil, then drop the heat to medium and let simmer for about 15 minutes, until the mixture is reduced down to a syrup. Turn off the heat and pour that sizzurp into a large mixing bowl.

2 **For the fritters:** In a large mixing bowl, whisk together the milk, egg, energy drink, Jager, flour, cornmeal, sugar, baking soda, and salt. Whisk it real good until it's nice and smooth.

3 Heat up the oil to 350°F in a Dutch oven, preferably cast iron. Your batter should be somewhere in between a liquid and a solid. I think my eighth-grade science teacher would have called it an amorphous solid. She would probably not approve of me making these. But who knows.

4 Use a serving spoon to scoop up about 2 tablespoons' worth of batter, then use your finger to slide it into the hot oil. There's no particular shape you're shooting for here, but rounder is better to ensure even cooking. Repeat to add about 12 more lumps. Make sure each fried lump gets evenly cooked by keeping them moving around in the oil.

5 When they're nice and golden brown, about 4 minutes, remove the crispy balls and let them drain on some paper towels. Drop those golden balls in the mixing bowl with the caffeinated Jager syrup and toss to coat. You want full syrup submergence. Pop those fritters onto a plate, dust with powdered sugar, and serve with a freshly poured Jager Bomb.

FRIED CHICKEN

SANDWICHES
with
Bacon Mayo

MAKES 4 SANDWICHES

4 slices bacon

2 tablespoons vinegar-based hot sauce

1 cup mayonnaise

½ head white cabbage

½ white onion

2 Fresno chilies

¼ cup apple cider vinegar

Salt

Black pepper

¼ cup chopped fresh dill

Fuckton of canola, vegetable, or peanut oil, for frying

4 cups flour

2 cups buttermilk

1 cup finely ground cornmeal

¼ cup Cajun seasoning

4 boneless skinless chicken thighs (about 3 ounces each)

4 circular buns (I still fuck with brioche, honestly)

Bunch of pickle slices

The first step you need to take for this recipe is to steel your nerves and prepare to lie. You are going to tell people that you made the bacon-fat mayo from scratch. You should probably call it aioli. I've made it from scratch before, emulsifying the melted bacon fat into egg yolks over a double boiler and all that, but I was batting like .350 on not completely fucking it up and soon decided it wasn't worth it. Now I just mix bacon and bacon fat and some other shit into store-bought mayo and then lie to people and tell them I made it. I suggest you do the same.

1   Heat a sauté pan on medium heat. Dice up your bacon as finely as possible, then drop it in the pan. Sauté for 10 to 12 minutes, until the bacon is fully rendered and crispy. Strain the fat into a bowl then pop it in the freezer for about 10 minutes. You want it to get to room temp. Run a knife through your bacon bits and turn them into bacon dust. Put the bacon dust in a bowl and whisk in your cooled bacon fat and the hot sauce and mayonnaise, then let it sit in the fridge.

2   Shred the cabbage as thinly as possible. Use a mandoline if you have one. Really, just get a mandoline. Send me an addressed envelope and I'll throw a Bed Bath & Beyond gift card your way or something. Slice your white onion thin. Slice your Fresno chilies thin. All thin everything. It's the Kate Moss of slaws.

3   In a large mixing bowl, combine the apple cider vinegar, 1 teaspoon salt, and ½ teaspoon black pepper and whisk together. Throw your slaw ingredients (cabbage, onion, Fresno) in there along with your dill, then toss to combine. Let the slaw hang out in the fridge while you fry chicken.

4   Heat your oil to 350°F in a Dutch oven, preferably cast iron. Set out three large mixing bowls: In the first, dump 2 cups of the flour; in the second, dump the buttermilk along with 1 teaspoon salt; in the third, dump the remaining 2 cups flour, the cornmeal, Cajun seasoning, and an additional 2 teaspoons salt.

5   Take the chicken thighs, wrap them loosely in plastic wrap, then beat them with any blunt object. Maybe work on your jab and punch them to thinness. You want them to be ½ inch thick at most.

6   Season up those chicken thighs with salt. Dredge them in the flour, then the buttermilk, then the flour-cornmeal mixture. Make sure to really pack the flour in at the last step.

7   Throw your chicken into the oil and fry for about 6 minutes, flipping halfway through if it looks like they aren't cooking evenly. They're done when the coating is a deep amber bordering on brown. Remove from the fryer and let drain on paper towels.

8   Toast up your buns. Spoon some bacon-y mayo on both sides of one, place a chicken thigh on the bottom bun, top it with a hefty handful of slaw and a few pickles, and go to work, big homie.

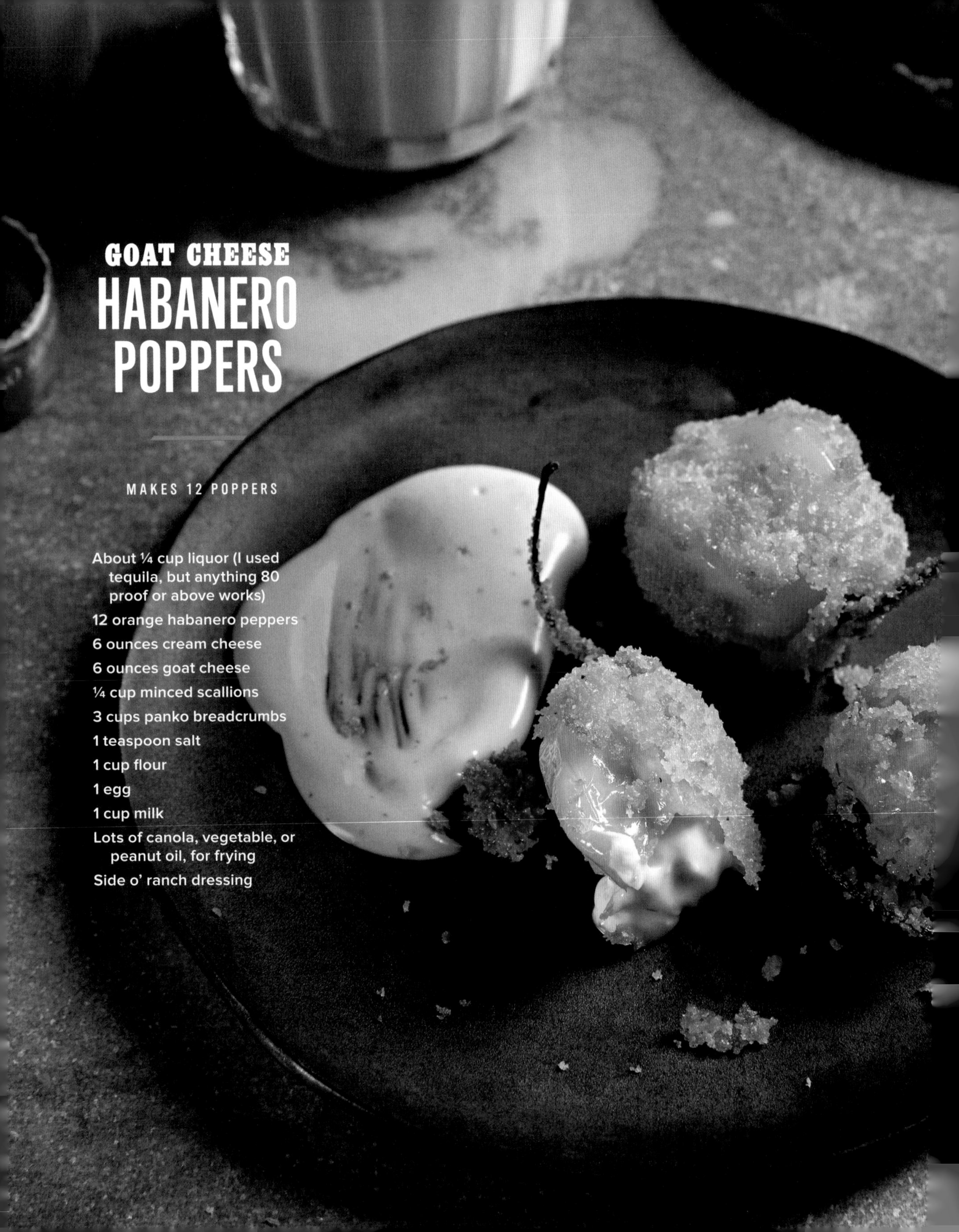

GOAT CHEESE
HABANERO
POPPERS

MAKES 12 POPPERS

About ¼ cup liquor (I used tequila, but anything 80 proof or above works)

12 orange habanero peppers

6 ounces cream cheese

6 ounces goat cheese

¼ cup minced scallions

3 cups panko breadcrumbs

1 teaspoon salt

1 cup flour

1 egg

1 cup milk

Lots of canola, vegetable, or peanut oil, for frying

Side o' ranch dressing

Habaneros are misrepresented in the media. Everyone just thinks of them as little orange butthole scorchers, but they're so much more. They're little orange butthole scorchers that taste really good. Habaneros have a piquant fruitiness to them that you don't get from that fresh-cut-grass flavor of jalapeños.

The only problem is, you can't enjoy the beautiful flavor without subjecting yourself to immense pain. That seems like a metaphor for something. I don't know what, but it's for sure something. I really wanted to make this recipe happen, because jalapeño poppers are my number-one-favorite bar snack (Buffalo wings would be number one if I could eat them with one hand) and habanero peppers are my number-one favorite pepper.

I'm pretty sure I found a way to make habaneros less hot, and it involves basic science and a pot of boiling tequila. I didn't exactly have perfect scientific control on the experiment, but I ate six of these and didn't die, so there's that.

1 OK cool, so you have to figure out a way to make these habaneros not kill you. Not an easy task! Start by getting a quart of water boiling in a saucepot. Since capsaicin dissolves in alcohol, blanching the chilies in liquored-up water is going to help tame the heat. So add your favorite hard liquor. The amount isn't really important. Set out a large mixing bowl and fill it with a bunch of ice cubes, then just enough water to cover the ice, but not too much.

2 Wear a pair of kitchen gloves so as not to fuck up your hands. Make an incision at the bottom of a habanero and make a slice that goes about halfway to the stem. Use a small paring knife to remove the seeds. Repeat. Throw about four of the habaneros into the boiling liquor water and let run for 10 seconds, then remove and toss in the ice bath. Be careful not to breathe near the pot because it will ruin your day. Repeat this process two times.

3 Mix together the cream cheese, goat cheese, and scallions in a small bowl. The cream cheese is going to give you that familiar creaminess, and that goat cheese is going to punch up the flavor with acid and funk. In case you had any questions about that. Oh, and this Chinese place near my house when I was a kid used to put scallions in their cream cheese wontons and they were dope.

4 Put the panko in a food processor along with the salt and let it run for 30 seconds, until super dusty. This is a good foolproof coating for fried shit. Put your panko in one bowl, fill another bowl with the flour, then another bowl with the egg and milk. Whisk them eggs and milk.

5 Heat your oil to 375°F in a Dutch oven, preferably cast iron.

6 Take the habaneros out of the ice bath, then dry them inside and out with paper towels, still wearing gloves. Spoon your cheese mix into the openings as best as you can. If you have a piping bag, use that, but you probably don't and neither do I. When the habaneros are sufficiently cheesed up, dredge in the flour, then in the egg wash, then in the panko mixture.

7 Drop into the fryer—work in batches so no poppers are touching in the oil—and fry away for about 1 minute, until the coating is golden brown and crispy. Pull them out and let drain on paper towels. Serve with ranch. You know, to cool it down. Because you're about to eat a dozen habaneros. Which is insane. By the way, maybe just take a small bite to make sure you're not gonna die...

SPICY
TUNA ROLL
CORN DOGS

MAKES 4 TUNA ROLL
CORN DOGS

Recipe Continues

You ever see the movie *Jiro Dreams of Sushi*? It's the one about the really old guy who makes the best sushi in the world and he dreams about it and he's really mean to his son or something and then there's a cool scene where people make sushi to orchestral music and it's very stylized and at the end there's a catharsis? It's really great. You should check it out sometime.

Anyways, the guy is so dialed in to his craft that he can tell if a sushi chef's hands are too warm or too cold just by the texture of the rice. The movie has several close-up shots of his face discerningly chewing tiny morsels of fish and rice to show you how dialed in he is. Whenever I make these spicy tuna corn dogs, I like to picture Jiro taking a bite in one of those super-slow-mo macro shots that would totally let you see the orange mayo and eel sauce dripping off his face. Then he discerningly chews, wipes his mouth with his pristine white chef's coat, smiles, and gives me a thumbs up. And we would call the movie *Josh Dreams of Jiro Dreaming of Sushi*. It would be followed by *Josh Dreams of Jiro Dreaming of Sushi II: The Streets*. It would go straight to On Demand.

4 uncut spicy tuna rolls from your cheapest local sushi joint (ask them to leave them uncut and they generally will)

Canola, vegetable, or peanut oil, for frying

¼ cup mayonnaise

1 tablespoon Sriracha

1 cup flour

1 cup yellow cornmeal

4 teaspoons baking powder

1 egg

1 cup ice-cold beer

1 tablespoon soy sauce

1 tablespoon honey

1 teaspoon sesame oil

¼ cup eel sauce

2 tablespoons furikake

1 Pop the sushi rolls in the freezer for at least half an hour. You want them to stay intact in the fryer and also not get too steamy while frying. Heat your oil to 350°F in a Dutch oven, preferably cast iron.

2 Whisk together the mayo and Sriracha. This is Sriracha mayo. Set it aside.

3 In a large mixing bowl, whisk together the flour, cornmeal, and baking powder. In a separate mixing bowl, combine the egg, beer, soy sauce, honey, and sesame oil and whisk that together. Then add the wet ingredients to the dry ingredients and whisk. This is corn dog batter, more or less.

4 Take your uncut sushi rolls out of the freezer, and fully submerge each into corn dog batter. Notice you're not putting a stick in them—yet. I tried to figure out a way to get the stick to stay in, but it won't. So this recipe is kind of a lie.

5 Drop two of your battered-up sushi dogs into the fryer; then, and this is important, use a spoon to continuously turn the rolls, which means the batter should coagulate in a perfectly circular fashion. Pull them out after about 3 minutes, when golden brown. Let drain on a paper towel. Repeat with the remaining dogs.

6 Jam a chopstick in the bottoms of the dick-shaped, oil-logged, culturally anachronistic monsters, then drizzle them with your Sriracha mayo and eel sauce and give them a dusting of furikake. Shove into your mouth-hole and enjoy.

MAC 'N' CHEESE
CHICHANGAS

MAKES 4 CHIMICHANGAS

Bunch of canola, vegetable, or peanut oil, for frying

1 large poblano pepper

6 strips bacon

1 tablespoon flour

2 cups whole milk

10 slices plastic-wrapped American cheese, torn into pieces

8 ounces sharp cheddar, shredded

1 teaspoon salt

½ teaspoon black pepper

½ pound macaroni noodles, cooked

4 large tortillas

Ranch dressing, for serving

It still baffles me how few chimichangas we eat as a society. It's probably a good thing considering everyone's fat and all. But, still, it seems suspicious that a food this good has been suppressed for this long. Neither Taco Bell nor Del Taco has a single chimichanga on their menu, and, even though Chipotle has a deep fryer on site, they won't drop your burrito in it, and their manager will be very rude and ask you to leave when you start screaming at the guy working the chip station.

I think we need to start converting more of our foods into deep-fried burritos. Doing it with a dope-ass poblano-and-bacon mac and cheese is a good gateway into the lifestyle, but don't stop there. Next time you're eating some tasty food, ask yourself: "Can I wrap this in a tortilla and fry it?" If the answer is yes, do it. If the answer is no, do it.

1 Heat your oil to 375°F in a Dutch oven, preferably cast iron. De-seed, de-stem, and de-stick your poblano. Give it a small dice. Also, dice up the bacon quite small.

2 Heat a large nonstick saucepot on medium heat and render your bacon for 5 minutes or so. When the bacon is no longer raw—but don't wait until it's super-crispy—add your poblano dice. Sauté for about 5 minutes, until the poblano is soft and the bacon is cooked.

3 Keeping the pan on medium heat, add the flour. Use a wooden spoon to combine and cook for 2 minutes. Add the milk and use a whisk to, eh, whisk it. Continuously whisk until the mixture has come up to a bubble. Add both of the cheeses, the salt, and the black pepper and keep whisking—never stop whisking—until the cheese is melted. Stir in the macaroni and continue to cook for another 2 minutes. You may have to add some more milk to loosen it up. Turn off the heat.

4 Heat a large nonstick pan on high heat. When it's adequately hot, throw in a tortilla. Let it griddle for about 10 seconds on both sides. Repeat. Keep the pan on medium heat. See why next!

5 Spoon a good amount of mac and/or cheese into the center of a tortilla, then roll it on up, making extra sure to tuck in the sides. Keep your fingers on the crease—where the tortilla ends its wrap—then place the crease down onto the hot pan. This is going to help seal it and eliminate your chances of dying in a not-so-freak chimichanga frying accident. (Chimichanga accidents take more lives every year than shark attacks. This is probably not true.) Repeat with the remaining tortillas and mac and cheese.

6 When all your burritos are properly burrito-ed, jam four or five toothpicks along the main tortilla fold and two toothpicks in each end to make sure it all holds together. Safety first!

7 One at a time, drop each one in the hot oil for about 30 seconds, until the tortilla becomes golden brown and starts to puff a bit. Pull out of the oil and let drain on paper towels. Serve with ranch. Serve most things with ranch, honestly. Fuckin' love ranch.

FUNNEL CAKE
BURGERS
with
Strawberry-
Rhubarb Ketchup

MAKES 4 BURGERS

Strawberry-Rhubarb Ketchup

2 tablespoons vegetable oil

1 cup minced rhubarb

½ cup minced strawberries

¼ cup warm water

2 tablespoons tomato paste

2 tablespoons cider vinegar

1 tablespoon Sriracha

1 tablespoon brown sugar

½ teaspoon smoked paprika

½ teaspoon cumin

1 teaspoon salt

½ teaspoon black pepper

Funnel Cakes

2 cups milk

1 egg

½ stick (4 tablespoons) butter, melted

2 cups flour

2 tablespoons grated pecorino

2 tablespoons minced chives

2 teaspoons smoked paprika

1 teaspoon baking soda

2 teaspoons salt

1 teaspoon black pepper

1 quart canola, vegetable, or peanut oil, for frying

Burgers

8 strips bacon

1½ pounds 80/20 ground beef

Salt to taste

Vegetable oil

4 slices white cheddar

Handful of wild arugula

This recipe makes sense. Every single part of it does and fuck you if you think it doesn't because you lack a basic understanding of logic and semantics. No, this is not the reason America is fat. The reason America's fat is because people like you think this is the reason America's fat while mindlessly sucking down a double cheeseburger with a large fry and a Big Gulp of Coke—which has more calories than this funnel cake burger—and thinking nothing of it. And it's not a burger covered in sugar; it's a savory funnel cake, you dick. Sorry, I still get really worked up about the whole funnel-cake-burger thing. This is one of the first recipes on my blog to blow up and then the trolls came.

▆▆▆▆▆▆▆▆▆▆▆▆▆▆▆▆▆▆▆▆▆▆▆

1 For the ketchup: Heat the vegetable oil in a small sauté pan on medium heat. When it starts to move around, add the rhubarb and strawberries and sauté for 3 minutes, mashing the strawberries a bit with a wooden spoon, until they've broken down considerably. Add the warm water, tomato paste, vinegar, Sriracha, sugar, paprika, cumin, salt, and pepper and whisk to combine. Let the mixture simmer for 5 or 6 minutes, until it's all reduced and looks like ketchup.

2 For the funnel cakes: Set out two large mixing bowls. Whisk the wet ingredients (milk, egg, and melted butter) in the first bowl, then whisk the dry ingredients (everything else except the oil) in the second. Then! Whisk the stuff from the two bowls together.

3 Heat the oil in a Dutch oven (preferably cast iron) until it reaches 375°F. Pour your batter into a sandwich bag and snip a ½-centimeter hole in the corner, or put it in one of those generic squirt bottles meant for condiments. Both work.

4 When the oil's hot, drip your batter in there in a steady stream, moving it back and forth in a random spiralized motion. Go Jackson Pollock on that motherfucker. Make a disc about 4 inches in diameter. After the batter turns golden brown on the bottom (about 1 minute), flip the funnel cake using some sort of stick—I always use chopsticks—then continue to cook for an additional 20 to 30 seconds on the other side, until golden brown on the other side. Remove and let drain on paper towels. Repeat the process to make seven more funnel buns.

5 For the burgers: Cook the bacon strips in a pan. Turn the pan on medium-high, put your bacon in, and cook it. Don't overthink this. It's bacon. Dry them on paper towels.

6 Form the beef into four even patties, then dust liberally with salt. Heat a large sauté pan on high heat with a few drops of vegetable oil. When the pan is smoking, sear your burgers on one side for about 4 minutes, until a nice crust develops. Then flip, add the cheese immediately, and cook for an additional 3 minutes, until the bottom has a hard sear on it.

7 Place a cheese-y meat disc on one funnel cake, top with 2 slices of bacon, a few leaves of arugula, and then drench that shit in your strawberry-rhubarb ketchup. Repeat.

DAMN, FIRST AND FOREMOST, I have to thank the team at Grand Central Life & Style, who used their first-round draft pick on an unproven rookie with a foul mouth and a bunch of really dumb ideas about food. Thank you to Tareth Mitch, Karen Murgolo, Elizabeth Turner, Deri Reed, Susan Benson Gutentag, and Nick Small for being the wheels that actually made this machine turn.

TO MY EDITOR, Morgan Hedden, who probably felt like she was wrangling a beauty pageant toddler after railing way too many lines of Pixie Stick dust while editing this insane brick of words. **TO MY AGENTS,** Steve Troha and Dado Derviskadic, AKA the Godfathers, for motivating me to get off my ass and actually do something with my life.

TO MY DESIGNER, Laura Palese, who had the difficult job of applying lipstick to this book-pig and made it look more beautiful than I could have imagined.

TO MY PHOTO TEAM: Photographer Andrea D'Agosto, food stylist Lauren Anderson, and prop stylist Alicia Buszczak. I had absolutely no idea what I was doing, and you all put the team on your backs. Shotgunning celebratory beers in the photo studio parking lot on wrap day was truly a highlight of my life. You're welcome for the tutorial, by the way.

TO ALL MY FRIENDS for being an extension of my family and for making me an extension of theirs. In no particular order, shout out to: Dip, Chad, Nick, Marcus, Rickards, Hannah, Elie, Geoff, Matt, Julian, Stam, Alex, Ramsey, Sammy, Alec, Emil, Sean, Dave, Daesong, Sander, Ryan, Kai, Dot, Julia, Kyle, Nicole, Thomas, Marielle, and all the people I'm forgetting. And a special friend shout out to Sammar and Natalia, who let me stage a house party at their apartment for the photo shoot. Sorry I ditched you guys without helping clean up. That was my bad.

TO MY BROTHER, JON: He taught me how to eat, he taught me how to drink, and he's been taste-testing my stupid-ass recipes for the better part of two decades. I truly never would have been able to pull this off without his lifelong support. **TO MY GIRLFRIEND, ANDREA:** She keeps me housed, clothed, loved, and I couldn't imagine anyone being a better mother to our cats.

ACKNOWLEDGMENTS

INDEX

ABOUT THE
Author

Josh Scherer is a food writer whose work has appeared in *Los Angeles* magazine, *LA Weekly*, *Eater*, *Food & Wine*, *Epicurious*, *Maxim*, *Thrillist*, *First We Feast*, and *Vice-Munchies*. He lives in Los Angeles with his girlfriend and two extremely shitty cats. When he's not making energy drink–infused BBQ sauces or whatever, he's probably getting schooled in basketball by 14-year-olds at a local park. He was a mediocre-at-best hammer thrower for UCLA's track-and-field team and an equally mediocre political science student. Likes Matt Damon movies. Hates celery.